MASTERING THE LINUX COMMAND LINE

Essential Commands and Tips for Beginners

THOMPSON CARTER

TABLE OF CONTENTS

INTRODUCTION

Mastering Linux Command Line Fundamentals

The Linux command line is a powerful tool that opens the door to a world of endless possibilities. Whether you are a beginner stepping into the realm of Linux for the first time or an experienced user looking to sharpen your skills, the command line is an essential part of the journey. This book, *Mastering the Linux Command Line: Essential Commands and Tips for Beginners*, serves as your comprehensive guide to understanding, navigating, and mastering the Linux command line environment.

Why Learn the Linux Command Line?

Linux is the backbone of modern computing, powering everything from personal computers and servers to cloud infrastructures and embedded systems. While graphical user interfaces (GUIs) provide simplicity and ease of use, they often lack the efficiency, flexibility, and control offered by the command line. Mastering the command line allows you to:

1. **Unlock Efficiency**:
    o   Automate repetitive tasks with scripts.
    o   Manage files and processes faster than GUI tools allow.

2. **Gain Deeper Control**:
   o Access system-level settings.
   o Monitor performance and troubleshoot issues in real-time.

3. **Work Across Diverse Environments**:
   o The command line is consistent across most Linux distributions, making your skills transferable to various systems.

4. **Enhance Career Prospects**:
   o Proficiency in Linux command line tools is a highly valued skill in IT, system administration, cloud computing, and software development.

What Makes This Book Unique?

This book is designed with beginners in mind, breaking down complex concepts into simple, jargon-free explanations. We emphasize real-world applications, ensuring that every command, example, and exercise is directly applicable to practical tasks you'll encounter. Here's what sets this book apart:

1. **Comprehensive Structure**:
   o The book is divided into 22 carefully curated chapters, each focusing on a key aspect of Linux

command line usage, from basic navigation to advanced scripting and security.

2. **Hands-On Approach**:
   o Each chapter includes real-world examples and exercises, encouraging you to practice as you learn.

3. **Practical Focus**:
   o Topics such as managing files, automating tasks, troubleshooting, and securing your system are presented with practical applications in mind.

4. **Expert Tips and Shortcuts**:
   o Discover tips, tricks, and shortcuts that seasoned Linux users rely on to boost productivity and efficiency.

5. **Beginner-Friendly Yet In-Depth**:
   o While the content is beginner-friendly, it doesn't shy away from exploring advanced concepts, ensuring you build a strong foundation and confidence.

What You'll Learn

By the end of this book, you'll have gained mastery over a wide range of Linux command line skills, including:

- Navigating and managing the Linux filesystem.

- Understanding users, groups, permissions, and access control.
- Installing, updating, and removing software using package managers.
- Networking basics and tools for connectivity and troubleshooting.
- Automating tasks with shell scripting.
- Managing system logs and debugging applications.
- Securing your system through SSH hardening, firewalls, and IP blocking.
- Optimizing workflows with aliases, customizations, and keyboard shortcuts.

You'll not only learn how to use commands but also understand their underlying principles, empowering you to tackle challenges confidently.

Who Is This Book For?

This book is tailored for:

1. **Beginners**:
   - If you are new to Linux or the command line, this book will guide you from the basics to more advanced topics at a comfortable pace.

2. **IT Professionals and Developers**:
   - Those working in IT, software development, or DevOps can use this book to solidify their Linux command line skills, which are indispensable in these fields.

3. **Students and Enthusiasts**:
   - Students pursuing computer science or related fields and enthusiasts exploring Linux for personal or professional growth will find this book an invaluable resource.

How to Use This Book

1. **Follow the Chapters in Order**:
   - The book is structured progressively, so each chapter builds on the knowledge from the previous one.

2. **Practice with Real-World Examples**:
   - Every chapter includes examples and exercises to help you apply what you've learned.

3. **Customize Your Learning**:
   - Explore expert tips and shortcuts to enhance your efficiency and tailor your learning experience.

4. **Refer to the Book as a Guide**:

- ○ Beyond completing the chapters, use this book as a reference manual whenever you encounter new challenges in the Linux command line.

Your Path Forward

This book is just the beginning of your Linux journey. Mastery of the command line opens doors to a deeper understanding of Linux systems, enabling you to explore areas such as system administration, cloud computing, cybersecurity, and development.

As you progress through this book, remember that the Linux command line is a skill honed through consistent practice and exploration. Embrace the challenges, experiment with new commands, and don't hesitate to revisit topics for deeper understanding.

Let's Begin

The command line is a gateway to unleashing the full potential of Linux. With this book, you'll not only learn how to navigate and use it effectively but also build the confidence to take on advanced tasks and projects. Whether you aim to enhance your career or satisfy your curiosity, this journey will equip you with the tools you need to succeed.

Let's dive in and start mastering the Linux command line!

CHAPTER 1: INTRODUCTION TO LINUX AND THE COMMAND LINE

1.1 Brief History and Evolution of Linux

The Origins of Linux

Linux traces its roots back to the early 1990s when **Linus Torvalds**, a Finnish student, developed the Linux kernel as a free, open-source alternative to proprietary operating systems like UNIX. Released in **1991**, the kernel provided a foundation for a modular operating system that could be freely modified and distributed.

- **UNIX Influence**: Linux borrowed heavily from UNIX, a powerful operating system developed in the 1970s at AT&T Bell Labs. While UNIX was proprietary, Linux embodied the open-source philosophy.
- **The GNU Project**: Founded by **Richard Stallman**, the GNU Project aimed to create a free UNIX-like operating system. Linux eventually filled the gap for the kernel, combining GNU tools with Linus Torvalds' kernel to form a complete operating system.

The Growth of Linux

Linux has evolved into a versatile platform used for:

- **Servers**: Most web servers today, including those of Google, Facebook, and Amazon, run on Linux.
- **Personal Computing**: Distributions like Ubuntu and Fedora make Linux accessible for desktop users.
- **Embedded Systems**: Linux powers devices like routers, smart TVs, and IoT gadgets.
- **Mobile**: Android, the dominant mobile operating system, is built on the Linux kernel.

1.2 Importance of the Command Line in Linux Systems

Why Learn the Command Line?

The command line interface (CLI) is the heart of Linux, offering unparalleled control, efficiency, and flexibility. While graphical user interfaces (GUIs) simplify many tasks, the CLI remains indispensable for:

1. **Control and Precision**:
   - CLI commands allow direct interaction with the operating system.
   - Tasks like managing files, editing configurations, and troubleshooting are faster and more precise on the command line.

2. **Resource Efficiency**:

- o CLIs consume fewer system resources than GUIs, making them ideal for servers and low-power devices.

3. **Automation**:
   - o CLI scripts can automate repetitive tasks, saving time and reducing errors.

4. **Ubiquity**:
   - o CLI skills are transferable across Linux distributions and are essential for managing remote servers where GUIs may not be available.

1.3 Differences Between GUI and CLI

Aspect	GUI	CLI
Ease of Use	Intuitive and beginner-friendly.	Requires learning commands and syntax.
Efficiency	Can be slower for repetitive tasks.	Faster for experienced users.
Resource Usage	High (requires graphics and memory resources).	Low (ideal for resource-constrained systems).
Automation	Limited automation	Extensive support for

Aspect	GUI	CLI
	options.	scripting.
Flexibility	Limited customization beyond what the GUI offers.	Highly customizable and extensible.
Accessibility	Often available locally.	Accessible locally or remotely via SSH.

Real-World Example

- **GUI**: A system administrator can use a file manager to copy files between directories, relying on drag-and-drop actions.
- **CLI**: The same task can be accomplished in seconds using the cp command:

bash

cp /path/to/source/file /path/to/destination/

1.4 Setting Up a Linux Environment

Choosing the Right Setup

To practice Linux, you can choose from several options based on your current system and needs:

1. **Virtual Machines (VMs)**:
   - Use tools like **VirtualBox** or **VMware** to install and run Linux within your existing operating system.
   - Pros: No need to modify your primary OS, easy to experiment with different distributions.
   - Cons: Performance depends on system resources.
   - Example: Installing Ubuntu on VirtualBox.

2. **Windows Subsystem for Linux (WSL)**:
   - For Windows users, WSL provides a lightweight Linux environment integrated with Windows.
   - Pros: No dual-booting required, seamless integration with Windows.
   - Cons: Limited hardware access compared to full Linux installations.
   - Example: Installing Ubuntu on WSL.

3. **Dual Boot**:
   - Install Linux alongside your existing operating system.
   - Pros: Full Linux experience with access to hardware resources.
   - Cons: Requires partitioning your hard drive; switching between systems requires a reboot.

4. **Live USB**:

   o Run Linux directly from a USB drive without installing it.

   o Pros: Great for testing Linux without changes to your system.

   o Cons: Limited persistence (data may not be saved after reboot).

Setting Up a Virtual Machine

1. Download VirtualBox from virtualbox.org.
2. Download a Linux ISO (e.g., Ubuntu) from the distribution's website.
3. Create a new virtual machine, allocate resources (RAM, storage), and attach the ISO to install Linux.

1.5 Understanding Terminal Emulators

What Is a Terminal Emulator?

A terminal emulator is a software application that provides a CLI interface, allowing users to interact with the operating system.

Popular Terminal Emulators

1. **GNOME Terminal**:

- o Default terminal on Ubuntu and other GNOME-based distributions.

2. **Konsole**:
   - o Default terminal for KDE Plasma desktop environments.

3. **xterm**:
   - o Lightweight and highly portable terminal emulator.

4. **Windows Terminal**:
   - o An advanced terminal for Windows users, supporting WSL.

Basic Components of a Terminal:

- **Prompt**: Displays information like the current user and directory (user@hostname:~$).
- **Cursor**: Indicates where the next command will be typed.
- **Input/Output**:
  - o Input: Commands typed by the user.
  - o Output: Results or feedback from the operating system.

How to Open a Terminal

- **Ubuntu**: Press Ctrl+Alt+T or search for "Terminal" in the application menu.
- **Fedora**: Use Alt+F2 and type gnome-terminal.

- **WSL**: Open the Windows Terminal and select your Linux distribution.

Real-World Exercise

Set Up a Linux Environment and Explore the CLI

1. Install a Linux distribution using your preferred method (VM, WSL, or Live USB).
2. Open a terminal and practice basic commands:
   - Display the current directory: pwd.
   - List files and directories: ls.
   - Navigate to a new directory: cd /path/to/directory.
3. Explore the filesystem hierarchy:
   - Navigate to /home and /etc.
   - Open a configuration file (e.g., /etc/hosts) using a text editor like nano.

This chapter introduced the Linux command line as an essential tool for system control and efficiency. You learned about Linux's history, the differences between GUI and CLI, and how to set up a Linux environment. With a terminal emulator ready, you're now prepared to start exploring the powerful commands and techniques that make Linux such a versatile operating system.

In the next chapter, you'll dive deeper into **Navigating the Filesystem**, understanding the Linux directory structure, and mastering the commands needed to explore it effectively.

CHAPTER 2: NAVIGATING THE FILESYSTEM

2.1 Basic Filesystem Structure and Hierarchy in Linux

What Is the Linux Filesystem?

The Linux filesystem is a tree-like hierarchical structure where the root directory (/) is the starting point. All files and directories stem from this root, making it easy to navigate and organize.

Key Directories in Linux

Directory	Purpose
/	Root directory. All other directories and files are nested within it.
/home	Contains personal directories for users (e.g., /home/username).
/etc	Stores configuration files for system and applications.
/var	Holds variable data like logs, caches, and runtime

Directory	Purpose
	files.
/usr	Contains user-installed software and libraries.
/bin and /sbin	Store essential binary executables (e.g., ls, pwd, cd).
/dev	Contains device files representing hardware components (e.g., /dev/sda).
/tmp	Temporary files created by programs and the system.

2.2 Using Basic Navigation Commands

2.2.1 The pwd Command

The pwd (print working directory) command displays the current directory in the filesystem.

Usage:

bash

pwd
Output Example:

bash

/home/username

2.2.2 The ls Command

The ls (list) command displays the contents of a directory.

Common Options:

- ls: Lists files and directories in the current location.
- ls -l: Displays detailed information, including permissions, ownership, and file size.
- ls -a: Lists all files, including hidden files (those starting with .).
- ls -lh: Shows file sizes in a human-readable format (e.g., MB, GB).

Usage Examples:

bash

ls
ls -l
ls -a
ls -lh /etc
Output Example:

bash

drwxr-xr-x 2 root root 4096 Nov 23 10:00 config/
-rw-r--r-- 1 root root 2048 Nov 22 08:15 sample.txt

2.2.3 The cd Command

The cd (change directory) command allows you to navigate to a different directory.

Common Usage:

- cd /path/to/directory: Navigate to a specific directory.
- cd ~: Shortcut to the user's home directory.

- cd ..: Move up one level in the directory hierarchy.
- cd -: Switch to the previous working directory.

Examples:

bash

cd /home/username
cd ~
cd ..
cd /etc

Tips:

- Use tab for auto-completion when typing directory or file names.
- Combine ls and cd for faster navigation:

    bash

    cd $(ls -d */ | grep target-folder)

2.3 Real-World Example: Navigating to a Specific Directory and Listing Its Contents

Scenario:

You need to navigate to the /var/log directory to check system logs.

Steps:

1. Use pwd to confirm your current location.

    bash

    pwd

Example output:

bash

/home/username

2. Change to the /var/log directory using cd.

bash

cd /var/log

3. Verify your new location using pwd.

bash

pwd
Output:

bash

/var/log

4. List the contents of /var/log using ls -lh for detailed information.

bash

ls -lh
Example output:

bash

-rw-r--r-- 1 root root 10K Nov 22 09:10 boot.log
-rw-r--r-- 1 root root 30K Nov 22 08:15 syslog
drwxr-xr-x 2 root root 4K Nov 21 14:32 apache2/

5. If needed, move into the apache2 directory to check web server logs:

bash

cd apache2
ls -l

2.4 Exercise: Explore the /home and /etc Directories

Task 1: Navigate and List Contents of /home

1. Start in your current directory.
2. Use cd /home to navigate to the /home directory.
3. Use ls to list all user directories.
4. For each user directory, use ls -a to view hidden files.

Expected Output:

- You will see personal directories like /home/username and hidden files like .bashrc.

Task 2: Explore the /etc Directory

1. Use cd /etc to navigate to the /etc directory.
2. Use ls -lh to display the contents with detailed information.
3. Locate and identify:
   o Configuration files like hosts, passwd.
   o Directories like systemd, ssh.

Challenge:

Find the file containing the system's hostname:

1. Use cd and ls to navigate /etc.

2. Use grep to search for "hostname":

bash

grep "hostname" /etc/*

Key Tips for Efficient Navigation

- Use cd .. to quickly move up one directory.
- Use cd / to return to the root directory.
- Combine ls and grep to find specific files:

bash

ls | grep "config"

In this chapter, you explored the Linux filesystem structure and learned essential commands for navigating directories (pwd, ls, and cd). Mastering these commands is foundational to working efficiently on Linux systems. Through real-world examples and exercises, you practiced moving through directories and inspecting their contents.

In the next chapter, you'll dive into **Managing Files and Directories**, learning to create, move, rename, and delete files effectively.

CHAPTER 3: MANAGING FILES AND DIRECTORIES

3.1 Managing Files and Directories

3.1.1 Creating Files and Directories

Create Files: touch

The touch command creates an empty file or updates the timestamp of an existing file.

Syntax:

bash

touch filename

Examples:

bash

touch notes.txt

touch report1.txt report2.txt

Result: Creates notes.txt in the current directory or updates its modification time.

Create Directories: mkdir

The mkdir command creates one or more directories.

Syntax:

bash

mkdir directory_name

Examples:

bash

mkdir projects

mkdir projects/reports

mkdir -p projects/2024/Q1 # Create parent directories if they don't exist

Options:

- -p: Creates parent directories as needed.

3.1.2 Moving and Renaming Files and Directories

Move or Rename: mv

The mv command moves files/directories or renames them.

Syntax:

bash

mv source destination

Examples:

- **Move a file**:

  bash

  mv notes.txt /home/user/documents/
  Moves notes.txt to /home/user/documents/.

- **Rename a file**:

  bash

  mv old_name.txt new_name.txt

- **Move multiple files to a directory**:

  bash

mv *.txt /home/user/documents/

3.1.3 Copying Files and Directories

Copy: cp

The cp command copies files and directories.

Syntax:

bash

cp source destination

Examples:

- **Copy a file**:

  bash

  cp notes.txt backup_notes.txt

- **Copy multiple files**:

  bash

  cp *.txt /home/user/backup/

- **Copy directories**:

bash

cp -r projects backup_projects

The -r (recursive) option is required to copy directories.

3.1.4 Deleting Files and Directories

Delete Files: rm

The rm command removes files.

Syntax:

bash

rm filename

Examples:

bash

rm old_file.txt

rm report*.txt # Deletes all files matching the pattern

Delete Directories: rm -r

The -r (recursive) option is needed to delete directories.

Examples:

bash

rm -r old_project

rm -rf /tmp/backup # Force-delete without confirmation

Caution: Always verify the files and directories you delete, especially when using -rf.

3.2 Using Absolute vs. Relative Paths

Absolute Paths

An absolute path specifies the full path from the root directory (/).

Examples:

bash

cd /home/user/projects

ls /var/log

Relative Paths

A relative path specifies the location relative to the current directory.

Examples:

bash

cd ../reports # Move up one directory, then into "reports"

ls ./notes.txt # List "notes.txt" in the current directory

When to Use

- Use **absolute paths** for unambiguous locations or scripts.
- Use **relative paths** for quick navigation in specific contexts.

3.3 Real-World Example: Organizing Files in a Project Folder

Scenario:

You're managing a project that involves creating reports, storing resources, and archiving old files.

Steps:

1. **Create the Project Structure**:

   bash

   mkdir -p project/{reports,resources,archive}

2. **Add Files to the Structure**:

   bash

   touch project/reports/report1.txt
   touch project/resources/image1.png

3. **Move Files to Appropriate Locations**:

    bash

    mv image1.png project/resources/
    mv old_report.txt project/archive/

4. **Copy a Resource File**:

    bash

    cp   project/resources/image1.png
    project/resources/image1_backup.png

5. **Delete Obsolete Files**:

    bash

    rm project/archive/old_report.txt

6. **Verify Structure**:

    bash

    ls -R project/

3.4 Exercise: Create a Directory Tree for a Mock Project

Objective:

Create a directory structure for a mock project, populate it with files, and practice managing them.

Instructions:

1. Create the following directory structure:

   css

   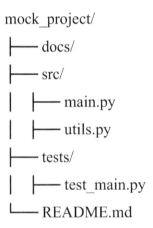

   ```
   mock_project/
   ├── docs/
   ├── src/
   │   ├── main.py
   │   ├── utils.py
   ├── tests/
   │   ├── test_main.py
   └── README.md
   ```

2. Use the following commands:
   o **Create directories**:

      bash

      mkdir -p mock_project/{docs,src,tests}

   o **Create files**:

bash

```
touch                    mock_project/src/main.py
mock_project/src/utils.py
touch mock_project/tests/test_main.py
touch mock_project/README.md
```

3. Perform the following tasks:
   o Move README.md to the docs folder.

   bash

   ```
   mv                    mock_project/README.md
   mock_project/docs/
   ```

   o Copy test_main.py to create test_utils.py in the tests folder.

   bash

   ```
   cp                    mock_project/tests/test_main.py
   mock_project/tests/test_utils.py
   ```

   o Delete the docs folder entirely.

   bash

rm -r mock_project/docs

4. Verify your work:

bash

ls -R mock_project/

Tips for Managing Files and Directories

- Use **wildcards** to work with multiple files:

bash

rm *.log # Delete all .log files
cp *.txt backup/

- Use ls -l and tree (if installed) to visualize directory structures:

bash

tree project/

- Always double-check paths when using destructive commands like rm or mv.

This chapter covered essential commands for creating, moving, renaming, copying, and deleting files and directories. You also learned the difference between absolute and relative paths and practiced organizing a project folder. Mastery of these commands will make your workflow efficient and structured.

In the next chapter, you'll explore **Understanding and Managing Permissions**, a critical aspect of Linux systems, to ensure security and proper access control.

CHAPTER 4: UNDERSTANDING AND MANAGING PERMISSIONS

4.1 Linux File Permissions Explained

Linux file permissions are a fundamental aspect of system security and functionality. They control who can access, modify, or execute files and directories.

4.1.1 The Permission Structure

Each file and directory in Linux has a set of permissions associated with three entities:

1. **Owner**: The user who owns the file.
2. **Group**: A group of users who have access to the file.
3. **Others**: All other users on the system.

The permission structure includes three types:

- **Read (r)**: Allows viewing the file contents.
- **Write (w)**: Allows modifying the file or directory.

- **Execute (x)**: Allows running a file as a program or accessing a directory.

4.1.2 Viewing Permissions

Use the ls -l command to view permissions.

Command:

bash

ls -l filename

Output Example:

bash

-rwxr-xr--

Breaking Down the Output:

Symbol Meaning

-       File type (- for file, d for directory).

rwx   Owner's permissions (read, write, execute).

r-x   Group's permissions (read, execute).

r--   Others' permissions (read only).

4.1.3 The Numeric Representation

Permissions can also be represented numerically:

- **Read (r)** = 4
- **Write (w)** = 2
- **Execute (x)** = 1

The numeric value is the sum of these:

- rwx = 7 (4+2+1)
- rw- = 6 (4+2)
- r-- = 4 (4+0+0)

Example:

- -rwxr-xr-- is 754.

4.2 Commands for Managing Permissions

4.2.1 Changing Permissions with chmod

The chmod command modifies file or directory permissions.

Syntax:

bash

chmod mode filename

Modes:

1. Symbolic:

   o   u: Owner

   o   g: Group

   o   o: Others

   o   a: All (owner, group, others)

   Example:

   bash

   chmod u+x script.sh # Add execute permission for owner

   chmod g-w file.txt   # Remove write permission for group

   chmod o=r file.txt   # Set others to read-only

2. Numeric: Example:

   bash

   chmod 755 script.sh # Set permissions to rwxr-xr-x

   chmod 644 file.txt   # Set permissions to rw-r--r--

4.2.2 Changing Ownership with chown

The chown command changes file ownership.

Syntax:

bash

chown user[:group] filename

Examples:

- Change owner:

  bash

  chown alice file.txt

- Change owner and group:

  bash

  chown alice:developers file.txt

4.2.3 Viewing Permissions with ls -l

The ls -l command displays detailed file information, including permissions, owner, and group.

Example:

bash

ls -l file.txt

Output:

bash

-rw-r--r-- 1 alice developers 1024 Nov 23 10:00 file.txt

4.3 Real-World Example: Securing a Script by Adjusting Permissions

Scenario:

You have created a shell script backup.sh that contains sensitive operations. Only you (the owner) should be able to execute it.

Steps:

1. **Create the Script**:

   bash

   touch backup.sh
   echo "echo 'Backing up files...'" > backup.sh

2. **Set Secure Permissions**:
   - o   Remove all access for group and others.
   - o   Ensure the owner can read, write, and execute.

   bash

chmod 700 backup.sh

3. **Verify Permissions**:

bash

ls -l backup.sh
Output:

bash

-rwx------ 1 username username 34 Nov 23 12:00 backup.sh

4. **Run the Script**:

bash

./backup.sh

5. **Test Access for Others**:
   - ○ Switch to another user (e.g., bob).
   - ○ Attempt to execute the script:

   bash

   su bob
   ./backup.sh

- o The system should deny access:

bash

permission denied: ./backup.sh

4.4 Exercise: Modify Permissions for Different Files and Test Access

Objective:

Practice setting and testing file permissions.

Instructions:

1. **Create the following files**:

bash

touch file1.txt file2.txt script.sh

2. **Set Permissions**:
   - o Allow the owner to read and write file1.txt, but no access for others:

bash

chmod 600 file1.txt

o   Allow everyone to read file2.txt, but only the owner can write:

bash

chmod 644 file2.txt

o   Make script.sh executable by the owner and group:

bash

chmod 750 script.sh

3. **Test Permissions**:

o   Switch to another user (e.g., bob) and attempt to read/write each file:

bash

su bob
cat file1.txt # Should deny access
echo "test" > file2.txt # Should deny write access
./script.sh # Should deny execute access

4. **Use ls -l to verify permissions**:

bash

ls -l

5. **Bonus Task**: Change the ownership of script.sh to the developers group:

bash

chown :developers script.sh

Tips for Managing Permissions

1. **Be Conservative with chmod**:
   o Avoid setting permissions to 777 unless absolutely necessary.
2. **Use chown Carefully**:
   o Ensure that sensitive files are not owned by untrusted users or groups.
3. **Test Before Deploying**:
   o Verify that your permissions allow only the intended access.

In this chapter, you learned how Linux file permissions work, how to view them with ls -l, and how to manage them using chmod and chown. You also applied these concepts to secure a script and tested access control.

In the next chapter, you'll dive into **Viewing and Editing Files**, exploring commands and tools for efficiently reading, modifying, and saving text files in Linux.

CHAPTER 5: VIEWING AND EDITING FILES

5.1 Commands to Display File Contents

Linux provides various commands to view file contents, each suited for specific use cases. Whether you need a quick glance at a file, to navigate large files, or to extract specific lines, these commands have you covered.

5.1.1 Viewing Files with cat

The cat command displays the entire content of a file in one go.

Syntax:

bash

cat filename

Examples:

- Display a file:

  bash

  cat notes.txt

- Concatenate and display multiple files:

  bash

  cat file1.txt file2.txt

Limitations:

- Not ideal for large files as the output can quickly overwhelm the terminal.

5.1.2 Viewing Files Page by Page with less

The less command lets you scroll through a file one page at a time.

Syntax:

bash

less filename

Navigation:

- Press Space to scroll down.
- Press b to scroll up.
- Press q to quit.

Example:

bash

less /var/log/syslog

5.1.3 Scrolling Through Files with more

The more command is similar to less, but with fewer navigation features.

Syntax:

bash

more filename

Navigation:

- Press Enter to scroll line by line.
- Press Space to scroll page by page.
- Press q to quit.

Example:

bash

more report.txt

5.1.4 Viewing the Start of a File with head

The head command shows the first few lines of a file (10 lines by default).

Syntax:

bash

head filename

Options:

- Display a specific number of lines:

    bash

    head -n 5 filename

Example:

bash

head /etc/passwd

5.1.5 Viewing the End of a File with tail

The tail command shows the last few lines of a file (10 lines by default).

Syntax:

bash

tail filename

Options:

- Display a specific number of lines:

  bash

  tail -n 15 filename

- Monitor a file in real-time:

  bash

  tail -f /var/log/syslog

Example:

bash

tail -f /var/log/syslog

5.2 Introduction to Text Editors

In Linux, text editors are essential tools for creating and modifying files. The two most commonly used editors are **nano** and **vim**.

5.2.1 Nano: A Beginner-Friendly Editor

Nano Basics: Nano is a straightforward, easy-to-use text editor ideal for beginners.

Command to Open Nano:

bash

nano filename

Key Shortcuts:

- **Save Changes**: Ctrl + O (Write Out)
- **Exit**: Ctrl + X
- **Search**: Ctrl + W
- **Cut Text**: Ctrl + K
- **Paste Text**: Ctrl + U

Example:

- Open or create a file:

  bash

nano notes.txt

- Add text, save with Ctrl + O, and exit with Ctrl + X.

5.2.2 Vim: A Powerful Editor for Advanced Users

Vim Basics: Vim is a robust text editor with powerful features, but it has a steeper learning curve.

Command to Open Vim:

bash

vim filename

Modes in Vim:

1. **Normal Mode** (default): For navigation and commands.
2. **Insert Mode**: For editing text (enter with i).
3. **Command Mode**: For saving, quitting, etc. (enter with :).

Key Commands:

- Switch to Insert Mode: Press i.
- Save and Exit: Press Esc, then :wq.
- Quit Without Saving: Press Esc, then :q!.
- Delete a Line: Press dd.

Example:

- Open a file:

bash

vim config.txt

- Edit text, then save and exit.

5.3 Real-World Example: Editing a Configuration File with Nano

Scenario:

You need to modify the hosts file to add a custom domain mapping for testing purposes.

Steps:

1. **Open the File**:

bash

sudo nano /etc/hosts

2. **Add the Custom Mapping**:
   - o   Scroll to the end of the file and add:

lua

127.0.0.1   test.local

3. **Save Changes**:
    o   Press Ctrl + O, then Enter to save.
4. **Exit Nano**:
    o   Press Ctrl + X.
5. **Verify Changes**:
    o   Check the file content:

    bash

    cat /etc/hosts

5.4 Exercise: Create and Edit a Plain Text File

Objective:

Create a plain text file, edit its contents using nano and vim, and practice viewing it with various commands.

Instructions:

1. **Create a New File**:

    bash

touch my_notes.txt

2. **Edit the File with Nano**:
   - o Open the file:

     bash

     nano my_notes.txt

   - o Add the following text:

     diff

     To-Do List:
     - Learn Linux commands.
     - Practice shell scripting.
     - Explore text editors.

   - o Save and exit.

3. **View the File**:
   - o Display its content with cat:

     bash

     cat my_notes.txt

   - o View the first two lines with head:

bash

head -n 2 my_notes.txt

- o View the last line with tail:

bash

tail -n 1 my_notes.txt

4. **Edit the File with Vim**:
   - o Open the file:

bash

vim my_notes.txt

- o Add a new line at the end:

diff

- Customize the environment.

- o Save and exit (:wq).

5. **Monitor Changes in Real-Time**:
   - o Open a second terminal and run:

bash

tail -f my_notes.txt

    o   Add another line to the file using nano, and watch the update appear in the first terminal.

Tips for Viewing and Editing Files

1. Use less for large files:

bash

less /var/log/syslog

2. For quick edits, use nano. For complex tasks, explore vim.
3. Use tail -f for real-time monitoring of log files.
4. Always double-check file paths when editing sensitive files like those in /etc.

In this chapter, you learned various commands for viewing file contents (cat, less, more, head, tail) and how to edit files using **nano** and **vim**. You applied these skills to edit a configuration file and performed hands-on exercises to solidify your understanding.

In the next chapter, you'll explore **Searching and Finding Files**, where you'll learn how to locate files and search their contents efficiently using commands like find, locate, and grep.

CHAPTER 6: SEARCHING AND FINDING FILES

6.1 Finding Files with Linux Commands

Efficiently locating files is crucial for managing and troubleshooting Linux systems. Linux provides several powerful tools to search for files based on various criteria.

6.1.1 The find Command

The find command searches for files and directories recursively based on specified conditions.

Syntax:

bash

find [path] [criteria] [action]

Common Options:

- -name: Search by file name.
- -type: Search by file type (f for files, d for directories).

- -mtime: Search for files modified within a specified number of days.
- -size: Search by file size.

Examples:

- Find a file named notes.txt:

  bash

  find /home -name "notes.txt"

- Find all .log files in /var:

  bash

  find /var -name "*.log"

- Find files modified in the last 7 days:

  bash

  find /home -mtime -7

- Find files larger than 10MB:

  bash

find /home -size +10M

6.1.2 The locate Command

The locate command uses a prebuilt index to quickly find files.

Syntax:

bash

locate [filename]

Examples:

- Find all files containing "config":

  bash

  locate config

Updating the Index: To ensure accurate results, update the index periodically:

bash

sudo updatedb

6.1.3 The which Command

The which command locates the executable path of a command or program.

Syntax:

bash

which [command]

Examples:

- Find the location of the python3 binary:

  bash

  which python3

- Check where grep is installed:

  bash

  which grep

6.2 Searching File Contents with grep

The grep command searches for specific patterns within files.

Syntax:

bash

grep [options] "pattern" filename

Common Options:

- -i: Case-insensitive search.
- -n: Display line numbers.
- -r: Search recursively in directories.
- --color: Highlight matching text.

Examples:

- Search for "error" in syslog:

  bash

  grep "error" /var/log/syslog

- Search for "failed" in all .log files in a directory:

  bash

  grep "failed" /var/log/*.log

- Search recursively for "TODO" in the current directory:

  bash

grep -r "TODO" .

6.3 Real-World Example: Searching Logs for Errors Using grep

Scenario:

You need to investigate system logs for error messages to troubleshoot an issue.

Steps:

1. **Navigate to the Logs Directory**:

   bash

   cd /var/log

2. **Search for Errors in the System Log**:

   bash

   grep -i "error" syslog

3. **View Line Numbers for Context**:

   bash

grep -in "error" syslog

4. **Highlight and Display Matches in Multiple Log Files**:

   bash

   grep --color -i "error" *.log

5. **Refine Results with Piping**:
   - Only display lines containing "critical":

   bash

   grep -i "error" syslog | grep -i "critical"

6.4 Exercise: Find Files Modified in the Last 7 Days

Objective:

Practice using the find command to locate recently modified files.

Instructions:

1. **Search in Your Home Directory**:

   bash

   find ~/ -mtime -7

2. **Search for .txt Files Modified in the Last 7 Days**:

bash

```
find ~/ -name "*.txt" -mtime -7
```

3. **Refine Results to Show Only Files Larger than 1MB**:

bash

```
find ~/ -mtime -7 -size +1M
```

4. **Bonus Task**:

   o   Save the list of results to a file for review:

   bash

```
find ~/ -mtime -7 > recent_files.txt
```

Tips for Efficient Searching

1. **Combine find with Actions**:

   o   Automatically delete files older than 30 days:

   bash

```
find /tmp -mtime +30 -delete
```

2. **Combine grep with Other Commands**:
   - ○ Search compressed log files:

     bash

     zgrep "error" /var/log/syslog.gz

3. **Use Aliases for Frequent Searches**:
   - ○ Add the following to your .bashrc or .zshrc for quick error searches:

     bash

     alias findlogs='grep -i "error" /var/log/*.log'

4. **Update the locate Index Regularly**:

   bash

   sudo updatedb

This chapter covered essential tools for searching files (find, locate, which) and their contents (grep). You practiced locating files modified within a specific timeframe and searching logs for error messages. These skills are invaluable for troubleshooting, managing large systems, and quickly locating important data.

In the next chapter, you'll explore **Working with Archives and Compressed Files**, learning how to compress, extract, and manage file archives with commands like tar, gzip, and bzip2.

CHAPTER 7: WORKING WITH ARCHIVES AND COMPRESSED FILES

7.1 Compressing and Decompressing Files

File compression is a common practice to save storage space and make file transfers more efficient. Linux provides powerful tools like tar, gzip, and bzip2 for creating and managing compressed files.

7.1.1 The tar Command

The tar command is used to create, extract, and manage file archives. It does not compress files by itself but is often combined with compression utilities.

Syntax:

bash

tar [options] [archive_name.tar] [files/directories]

Common Options:

- -c: Create an archive.
- -x: Extract an archive.
- -v: Verbose mode (shows progress).
- -f: Specify the archive file name.
- -t: List the contents of an archive.

Examples:

- Create an archive:

  bash

  tar -cvf archive.tar file1.txt file2.txt

- Extract an archive:

  bash

  tar -xvf archive.tar

- List the contents of an archive:

  bash

  tar -tvf archive.tar

7.1.2 The gzip Command

The gzip command compresses files using the Gzip algorithm, reducing their size significantly.

Syntax:

bash

gzip [filename]

Common Options:

- -d: Decompress a file.
- -k: Keep the original file after compression.

Examples:

- Compress a file:

  bash

  gzip file.txt
  Result: file.txt.gz

- Decompress a file:

  bash

gzip -d file.txt.gz

- Compress a tar archive:

bash

tar -cvf archive.tar file1.txt file2.txt
gzip archive.tar
Result: archive.tar.gz

7.1.3 The bzip2 Command

The bzip2 command compresses files more effectively than gzip, but it is slower.

Syntax:

bash

bzip2 [filename]

Common Options:

- -d: Decompress a file.
- -k: Keep the original file after compression.

Examples:

- Compress a file:

bash

bzip2 file.txt

Result: file.txt.bz2

- Decompress a file:

bash

bzip2 -d file.txt.bz2

7.2 Creating and Extracting Archives

7.2.1 Combining tar with Compression

The tar command can directly compress archives using gzip or bzip2.

Gzip Compression:

bash

tar -czvf archive.tar.gz file1.txt file2.txt

Bzip2 Compression:

bash

tar -cjvf archive.tar.bz2 file1.txt file2.txt

Extracting Compressed Archives:

- Extract .tar.gz:

  bash

  tar -xzvf archive.tar.gz

- Extract .tar.bz2:

  bash

  tar -xjvf archive.tar.bz2

7.2.2 Compressing Directories

To compress entire directories:

bash

tar -czvf project_backup.tar.gz /path/to/project

7.2.3 Extracting Specific Files

To extract only certain files from an archive:

bash

tar -xvf archive.tar.gz file1.txt file2.txt

7.3 Real-World Example: Backing Up and Compressing a Project Directory

Scenario:

You need to back up a project directory, compress it, and ensure it can be restored when needed.

Steps:

1. **Navigate to the Directory**:

   bash

   cd /path/to/project

2. **Create a Compressed Archive**:

   bash

   tar -czvf project_backup.tar.gz /path/to/project

3. **Verify the Archive**:
   o   List its contents:

   bash

   tar -tvf project_backup.tar.gz

4. **Move the Backup to a Safe Location**:

bash

mv project_backup.tar.gz /backup/location

5. **Extract the Archive**:
    o   Restore the project to another location:

    bash

    tar -xzvf project_backup.tar.gz -C /new/location

7.4 Exercise: Create and Extract Tar Archives

Objective:

Practice creating, compressing, and extracting archives.

Instructions:

1. **Create a Directory Structure**:
    o   Create a mock project directory:

    bash

    mkdir -p project/{docs,src,tests}
    touch   project/docs/readme.txt   project/src/main.py
    project/tests/test_main.py

2. **Create a Tar Archive**:
   - o Archive the project directory:

     bash

     tar -cvf project.tar project

3. **Compress the Archive**:
   - o Use gzip:

     bash

     gzip project.tar

   - o Verify the compressed file:

     bash

     ls -lh project.tar.gz

4. **Extract the Archive**:
   - o Decompress the file:

     bash

     gzip -d project.tar.gz

   - o Extract the tar archive:

bash

tar -xvf project.tar

5. **Bonus Task**:
   o Create a .tar.bz2 archive:

   bash

   tar -cjvf project.tar.bz2 project

Tips for Working with Archives

1. **Check Before Extracting**:
   o Use tar -tvf to preview the archive contents before extraction.

2. **Exclude Files from Archives**:
   o Skip unnecessary files:

   bash

   tar   --exclude="*.log"   -cvf   archive.tar /path/to/directory

3. **Split Large Archives**:

- o Use the split command to divide large archives into smaller chunks:

bash

split -b 100M large_archive.tar.gz small_part_

4. **Compress in the Background**:
   - o For large directories, use nohup:

bash

nohup tar -czvf archive.tar.gz /large/directory &

Conclusion

In this chapter, you learned how to work with archives and compressed files using tar, gzip, and bzip2. You practiced creating, compressing, and extracting archives, and applied these skills to back up a project directory. Mastering these tools is essential for efficient file management, backups, and storage optimization.

In the next chapter, you'll explore **Managing Processes**, learning how to monitor, control, and terminate processes effectively using commands like ps, top, and kill.

CHAPTER 8: MANAGING PROCESSES

8.1 Understanding Processes and Their States

What Are Processes?

A process is an instance of a running program. In Linux, every task executed by the system, whether initiated by a user or running in the background, is a process.

Types of Processes:

1. **Foreground Processes**:
   - o Run in the terminal window.
   - o Can interact directly with the user.
   - o Example: Running a Python script.

2. **Background Processes**:

- o Run without user interaction.
- o Continue to execute even if the terminal is closed (if detached).
- o Example: A web server.

Process States:

Processes can exist in various states:

- **Running (R)**: Actively executing on the CPU.
- **Sleeping (S)**: Waiting for an event (e.g., user input or resource availability).
- **Stopped (T)**: Halted, usually by a signal (e.g., Ctrl+Z).
- **Zombie (Z)**: Completed execution but not yet removed by the parent process.

8.2 Commands for Managing Processes

Linux provides powerful commands for monitoring and controlling processes.

8.2.1 Viewing Processes with ps

The ps command displays information about running processes.

Syntax:

bash

ps [options]

Common Options:

- -e: Show all processes.
- -f: Show detailed information.
- aux: Display all processes with user and memory details.

Examples:

- View all processes:

    bash

    ps -e

- View detailed information:

    bash

    ps -ef

- View processes for the current user:

    bash

    ps aux

Output Fields:

- **PID**: Process ID, used to identify the process.
- **TTY**: Terminal associated with the process.
- **CMD**: Command that started the process.

8.2.2 Monitoring Processes with top and htop

The top Command

The top command provides a real-time, dynamic view of processes.

Command:

bash

top

Key Information:

- CPU and memory usage.
- PID and owner of processes.
- System load averages.

Navigation:

- Press q to quit.
- Press k and enter a PID to kill a process.

The htop Command

htop is an interactive, user-friendly alternative to top.

Command:

bash

htop

Features:

- Easier navigation with arrow keys.
- Search for processes (F3).
- Kill processes interactively (F9).

Install htop:

bash

sudo apt install htop # For Debian/Ubuntu
sudo yum install htop # For RHEL/CentOS

8.2.3 Controlling Processes with kill

The kill command sends signals to processes to control their behavior.

Syntax:

bash

kill [signal] PID

Common Signals:

- SIGTERM (15): Politely requests the process to terminate.
- SIGKILL (9): Forces the process to terminate immediately.
- SIGHUP (1): Restarts a process.

Examples:

- Terminate a process:

  bash

  kill 1234 # Where 1234 is the PID

- Force-terminate a process:

  bash

  kill -9 1234

8.2.4 Managing Jobs with jobs

The jobs command displays processes started in the current terminal.

Syntax:

bash

jobs

Output:

- Each job has a unique ID (denoted by %).
- Example:

  bash

  [1]+ Running   ./long_script.sh &

Controlling Jobs:

- Bring a job to the foreground:

  bash

  fg %1

- Send a job to the background:

  bash

  bg %1

8.3 Real-World Example: Terminating an Unresponsive Application

Scenario:

A web browser has become unresponsive, and you need to terminate it.

Steps:

1. **List All Running Processes**:

   bash

   ps aux

   Look for the browser's name (e.g., firefox) and note its PID.

2. **Use kill to Terminate the Process**:

   bash

   kill 1234

   Replace 1234 with the actual PID.

3. **If the Process Does Not Respond**:
   o   Force terminate it:

   bash

kill -9 1234

4. **Verify That the Process Has Ended**:

bash

ps aux | grep firefox

8.4 Exercise: Identify and Stop a Specific Process by Its PID

Objective:

Practice identifying and terminating processes using their PID.

Instructions:

1. **Start a Background Process**:
   o Open a new terminal and run:

   bash

   sleep 300 &

   o Note the job number (e.g., [1]).
2. **List Running Processes**:
   o Use ps to find the PID of the sleep process:

   bash

ps aux | grep sleep

3. **Terminate the Process**:
   - o   Use kill to stop the process:

   bash

   kill <PID>

   - o   Replace <PID> with the actual process ID.

4. **Verify That the Process Has Ended**:
   - o   Check with:

   bash

   ps aux | grep sleep

5. **Bonus Task**:
   - o   Start another process (e.g., ping google.com) and practice managing it using jobs, fg, and bg.

Tips for Managing Processes

1. **Avoid Force-Terminating Critical Processes**:
   - o   Use SIGTERM first before resorting to SIGKILL.

2. **Monitor Resource-Intensive Processes**:

   o Use top or htop to identify and troubleshoot processes consuming excessive CPU or memory.

3. **Log Long-Running Processes**:

   o Redirect output to a log file to debug issues:

   bash

   ./script.sh > output.log 2>&1 &

4. **Automate Process Monitoring**:

   o Use tools like cron to periodically log running processes:

   bash

   ps aux > /tmp/process_log.txt

This chapter introduced you to processes, their states, and essential tools (ps, top, htop, kill, jobs) for managing them. You learned to identify, monitor, and terminate processes efficiently, with a real-world example demonstrating how to stop an unresponsive application.

In the next chapter, you'll explore **Understanding Linux Users and Groups**, delving into user management, permissions, and group-based access control to further enhance your command-line skills.

CHAPTER 9: UNDERSTANDING LINUX USERS AND GROUPS

9.1 Introduction to Linux Users and Groups

Linux is a multi-user operating system, meaning multiple users can interact with the system simultaneously. Users and groups are critical for managing access and permissions, ensuring security, and organizing resources.

Key Concepts:

- **Users**:
  - Each user has a unique username and ID (UID).
  - Users can own files and processes, with specific permissions.
- **Groups**:
  - Groups are collections of users.
  - Permissions can be assigned to groups, enabling shared access to resources.

User and Group Files:

1. /etc/passwd: Stores user account details.
2. /etc/shadow: Stores encrypted user passwords.
3. /etc/group: Stores group information.

9.2 Managing Users

9.2.1 Adding Users with useradd

The useradd command creates new users.

Syntax:

bash

sudo useradd [options] username

Common Options:

- -m: Create a home directory for the user.

- -s: Specify the user's default shell (e.g., /bin/bash).
- -G: Assign the user to one or more groups.

Examples:

- Add a user and create their home directory:

  bash

  sudo useradd -m alice

- Add a user with a specific shell:

  bash

  sudo useradd -m -s /bin/bash bob

9.2.2 Modifying Users with usermod

The usermod command changes user account settings.

Syntax:

bash

sudo usermod [options] username

Common Options:

- -G: Add the user to additional groups.
- -L: Lock the user's account.

- -U: Unlock the user's account.

Examples:

- Add a user to the developers group:

  bash

  sudo usermod -aG developers alice

- Lock a user account:

  bash

  sudo usermod -L alice

9.2.3 Setting Passwords with passwd

The passwd command sets or changes a user's password.

Syntax:

bash

sudo passwd username

Example:

- Set a password for alice:

bash

sudo passwd alice

9.2.4 Deleting Users with userdel

The userdel command removes user accounts.

Syntax:

bash

sudo userdel [options] username

Common Options:

- -r: Remove the user's home directory and mail spool.

Examples:

- Delete a user but keep their files:

  bash

  sudo userdel bob

- Delete a user and their home directory:

  bash

sudo userdel -r bob

9.3 Managing Groups

9.3.1 Adding Groups with groupadd

The groupadd command creates new groups.

Syntax:

bash

sudo groupadd groupname

Example:

- Create a group named developers:

    bash

    sudo groupadd developers

9.3.2 Modifying Groups with groupmod

The groupmod command changes group properties.

Syntax:

bash

sudo groupmod [options] groupname

Common Options:

- -n: Rename a group.

Example:

- Rename the developers group to engineers:

  bash

  sudo groupmod -n engineers developers

9.3.3 Deleting Groups with groupdel

The groupdel command removes groups.

Syntax:

bash

sudo groupdel groupname

Example:

- Delete the engineers group:

  bash

  sudo groupdel engineers

9.4 Real-World Example: Adding a New User and Setting Permissions

Scenario:

You want to add a new user named john, assign them to the developers group, and give them access to a shared directory.

Steps:

1. **Add the New User**:

    bash

    ```
    sudo useradd -m -s /bin/bash john
    sudo passwd john
    ```

2. **Create the Group**:

    bash

    ```
    sudo groupadd developers
    ```

3. **Add john to the Group**:

    bash

    ```
    sudo usermod -aG developers john
    ```

4. **Create a Shared Directory**:

bash

sudo mkdir /shared/developers

sudo chown :developers /shared/developers

sudo chmod 770 /shared/developers

5. **Verify Access**:
   - ○ Log in as john and check access to /shared/developers.

9.5 Exercise: Create a New Group and Add Users to It

Objective:

Create a new group and add multiple users to it.

Instructions:

1. **Create a New Group**:
   - ○ Name the group project_team:

     bash

     sudo groupadd project_team

2. **Add Users to the Group**:
   - ○ Add existing users alice and bob:

bash

sudo usermod -aG project_team alice
sudo usermod -aG project_team bob

3. **Verify Group Membership**:
   o Check group membership for alice and bob:

   bash

   groups alice
   groups bob

4. **Create a Shared Directory**:
   o Create /project/team_files:

   bash

   sudo mkdir /project/team_files

   o Set permissions:

   bash

   sudo chown :project_team /project/team_files
   sudo chmod 770 /project/team_files

5. **Test Access**:
   - o Log in as alice and confirm access to /project/team_files.

Tips for Managing Users and Groups

1. **Review Existing Users and Groups**:
   - o List all users:

     bash

     cat /etc/passwd

   - o List all groups:

     bash

     cat /etc/group

2. **Monitor User Logins**:
   - o View currently logged-in users:

     bash

     who

3. **Use Default Settings**:

   o   Ensure default home directories are created:

   bash

   sudo useradd -m username

In this chapter, you learned how to manage users and groups using commands like useradd, usermod, passwd, and groupadd. These tools are essential for controlling access and permissions in a multi-user Linux environment. You applied these skills in a real-world example and exercise, creating and managing users and groups effectively.

In the next chapter, you'll explore **Networking Basics**, learning to configure network settings and use commands like ping, ifconfig, and ssh.

CHAPTER 10: NETWORKING BASICS

10.1 Introduction to Networking in Linux

Networking is a core function of Linux systems, enabling communication between devices over a network. Linux provides powerful tools to view and manage network configurations, test connectivity, and transfer files.

10.2 Viewing Network Configuration

10.2.1 Using the ip Command

The ip command is a modern utility for network management, replacing the older ifconfig tool.

Syntax:

bash

ip [command] [options]

Common Commands:

- Display all network interfaces:

    bash

    ip addr

- Show only active interfaces:

    bash

    ip link show up

- Display routing table:

    bash

    ip route

Example:

bash

ip addr show eth0

Displays the IP address, subnet mask, and status of the eth0 interface.

10.2.2 Using the ifconfig Command

The ifconfig command is an older tool for network configuration, still available on many systems.

Syntax:

bash

ifconfig [interface]

Examples:

- Display all interfaces:

    bash

    ifconfig

- Bring an interface up:

    bash

sudo ifconfig eth0 up

- Bring an interface down:

bash

sudo ifconfig eth0 down

10.2.3 Testing Connectivity with ping

The ping command checks network connectivity by sending ICMP echo requests to a target.

Syntax:

bash

ping [options] hostname_or_IP

Common Options:

- -c: Specify the number of packets to send.

Examples:

- Test connectivity to google.com:

bash

ping google.com

- Send 5 packets:

bash

ping -c 5 google.com

Output:

- Shows packet loss, latency, and round-trip times.

10.3 Managing Connections

10.3.1 Connecting to a Remote Server with ssh

Secure Shell (SSH) is used to connect securely to remote servers over the network.

Syntax:

bash

ssh [user]@[hostname_or_IP]

Examples:

- Connect to a remote server:

bash

ssh alice@192.168.1.100

- Specify a custom port:

bash

ssh -p 2222 alice@192.168.1.100

- Use an identity file for authentication:

bash

ssh -i ~/.ssh/id_rsa alice@192.168.1.100

10.3.2 Transferring Files with scp

Secure Copy Protocol (SCP) is used to transfer files securely between systems.

Syntax:

bash

scp [source] [destination]

Examples:

- Copy a file to a remote server:

bash

scp file.txt alice@192.168.1.100:/home/alice/

- Copy a file from a remote server:

bash

scp   alice@192.168.1.100:/home/alice/file.txt
/local/directory/

- Copy an entire directory:

bash

scp -r project/ alice@192.168.1.100:/home/alice/

10.4 Real-World Example: Connecting to a Remote Server Using SSH

Scenario:

You want to connect to a remote server (192.168.1.50) as user john to manage files and configurations.

Steps:

1. **Check Network Connectivity**:

bash

ping -c 3 192.168.1.50

2. **Initiate the SSH Connection**:

bash

ssh john@192.168.1.50

3. **Authenticate**:
    - o Enter the password when prompted.
    - o If using an SSH key:

        bash

        ssh -i ~/.ssh/id_rsa john@192.168.1.50

4. **Execute Commands on the Remote Server**:
    - o List files:

        bash

        ls /home/john

5. **Exit the SSH Session**:

bash

exit

10.5 Exercise: Copy Files Between Systems Using SCP

Objective:

Practice transferring files securely between two Linux systems using SCP.

Instructions:

1. **Scenario**:
   - Your local system: 192.168.1.10.
   - Remote server: 192.168.1.20.
   - User on remote server: alice.

2. **Tasks**:
   - Copy a file (report.pdf) from your local system to the remote server:

   bash

   scp   report.pdf
   alice@192.168.1.20:/home/alice/documents/

   - Copy a directory (project) from the remote server to your local system:

   bash

```
scp    -r    alice@192.168.1.20:/home/alice/project/
/local/directory/
```

- o Verify the transferred files:
  - On the remote server:

```
bash
```

```
ssh alice@192.168.1.20
ls /home/alice/documents
```

  - On the local system:

```
bash
```

```
ls /local/directory/project
```

3. **Bonus Task**:
   - o Automate file transfers using a script:

```
bash
```

```
#!/bin/bash
scp                    -r                    /local/data/
alice@192.168.1.20:/remote/backup/
```

Tips for Networking

1. **Use ssh-copy-id to Simplify Authentication**:
   - o   Add your public key to the remote server:

     bash

     ssh-copy-id alice@192.168.1.20

2. **Monitor Network Traffic**:
   - o   Use iftop or nload to view real-time network usage:

     bash

     sudo apt install iftop
     sudo iftop

3. **Troubleshoot Network Issues**:
   - o   Use traceroute to diagnose routing problems:

     bash

     traceroute google.com

4. **Use rsync for Advanced File Transfers**:
   - o   Synchronize files between systems:

     bash

```
rsync                -av                /local/data/
alice@192.168.1.20:/remote/data/
```

In this chapter, you learned how to view network configurations using ip and ifconfig, test connectivity with ping, and manage connections with ssh and scp. These skills are essential for accessing remote systems, transferring files securely, and diagnosing network issues.

In the next chapter, you'll explore **Package Management**, learning how to install, update, and remove software using tools like apt and yum.

CHAPTER 11: PACKAGE MANAGEMENT

11.1 Introduction to Package Management

In Linux, software is typically distributed as packages, which are managed through package management tools. These tools simplify the installation, updating, and removal of software, ensuring that dependencies are correctly handled.

11.2 Common Package Managers

11.2.1 APT (Advanced Package Tool)

APT is the default package manager for Debian-based distributions, such as Ubuntu.

Common Commands:

- **Update Package Lists**:

  bash

  sudo apt update

- **Upgrade Installed Packages**:

  bash

  sudo apt upgrade

- **Install a Package**:

  bash

  sudo apt install package_name

- **Remove a Package**:

  bash

  sudo apt remove package_name

- **Search for a Package**:

bash

apt search package_name

11.2.2 YUM (Yellowdog Updater Modified)

YUM is a package manager for RHEL-based distributions like CentOS.

Common Commands:

- **Update Package Lists**:

  bash

  sudo yum check-update

- **Install a Package**:

  bash

  sudo yum install package_name

- **Remove a Package**:

  bash

  sudo yum remove package_name

- **List Installed Packages**:

  bash

  yum list installed

11.2.3 DNF (Dandified YUM)

DNF is a modern replacement for YUM, used in newer RHEL-based distributions like Fedora.

Common Commands:

- **Update Package Lists**:

  bash

  sudo dnf check-update

- **Install a Package**:

  bash

  sudo dnf install package_name

- **Remove a Package**:

  bash

sudo dnf remove package_name

- **Upgrade All Packages**:

bash

sudo dnf upgrade

11.3 Real-World Example: Installing and Removing a Software Package

Scenario:

You need to install the curl utility, use it, and then remove it from your system.

Steps Using APT (Ubuntu/Debian):

1. **Update the Package List**:

bash

sudo apt update

2. **Install curl**:

bash

sudo apt install curl

3. **Verify Installation**:
   o Check the version:

   bash

   curl --version

4. **Use curl**:
   o Fetch a webpage:

   bash

   curl https://example.com

5. **Remove curl**:

   bash

   sudo apt remove curl

Steps Using DNF (Fedora/RHEL):

1. **Update the Package List**:

   bash

sudo dnf check-update

2. **Install curl**:

bash

sudo dnf install curl

3. **Remove curl**:

bash

sudo dnf remove curl

11.4 Exercise: Update All Installed Packages on Your System

Objective:

Update all installed packages to their latest versions using your system's package manager.

Instructions:

1. **Update Package Lists**:
   o   For APT (Ubuntu/Debian):

   bash

   sudo apt update

- o   For YUM (CentOS/RHEL):

  bash

  sudo yum check-update

- o   For DNF (Fedora):

  bash

  sudo dnf check-update

2. **Upgrade All Installed Packages**:
   - o   For APT:

     bash

     sudo apt upgrade

   - o   For YUM:

     bash

     sudo yum update

   - o   For DNF:

     bash

sudo dnf upgrade

3. **Clean Up Unused Packages**:
   - For APT:

   bash

   sudo apt autoremove

   - For YUM:

   bash

   sudo yum autoremove

   - For DNF:

   bash

   sudo dnf autoremove

4. **Verify Updated Packages**:
   - For APT:

   bash

   apt list --upgradable

o   For YUM:

bash

yum list updates

o   For DNF:

bash

dnf list updates

11.5 Tips for Managing Packages

1. **Search for Packages**:
    o   Use the search feature to find a package before installing:

    bash

    apt search package_name

2. **Purge Configuration Files**:
    o   When removing a package, also remove its configuration files:

    bash

sudo apt purge package_name

3. **Enable Faster Downloads**:

   o   For APT, enable parallel downloads:

   bash

   sudo apt install apt-fast

4. **Enable Repositories**:

   o   For YUM/DNF, ensure necessary repositories are enabled:

   bash

   sudo   yum-config-manager   --enable repository_name

In this chapter, you learned to manage software using popular Linux package managers: APT, YUM, and DNF. You explored commands to install, update, and remove software packages, and practiced upgrading all installed packages on your system.

In the next chapter, you'll delve into **Shell Scripting**, learning how to automate tasks by writing and running custom scripts.

CHAPTER 12: UNDERSTANDING SHELLS AND SHELL SCRIPTING

12.1 What is a Shell, and Why Use Scripts?

What is a Shell?

A shell is a command-line interface (CLI) that interprets and executes user commands or scripts. It acts as a bridge between the user and the operating system.

- **Popular Shells**:
    - **Bash**: The default shell in many Linux distributions.
    - **Zsh**: A more feature-rich shell used by advanced users.

- o **Fish**: Known for its user-friendly syntax and features.

Why Use Shell Scripts?

A shell script is a text file containing a series of commands that can be executed sequentially. Scripts automate repetitive tasks, improve efficiency, and reduce errors.

Benefits:

- **Automation**: Perform tasks like backups, updates, or monitoring without manual intervention.
- **Efficiency**: Execute multiple commands with a single script.
- **Reproducibility**: Ensure consistent execution of tasks.

Common Use Cases:

- Backup automation.
- Log file analysis.
- Task scheduling.
- Application deployment.

12.2 Writing Your First Shell Script

Step 1: Create a Script File

1. Open a text editor (e.g., nano) to create a new file:

bash

nano my_script.sh

2. Add the **shebang** line at the top of the file:

bash

#!/bin/bash

   o The shebang specifies the interpreter (in this case, Bash) to execute the script.

Step 2: Add Commands

Add a series of commands to the script:

bash

```
#!/bin/bash
echo "Hello, World!"
echo "Today is $(date)"
echo "System uptime: $(uptime -p)"
```

Step 3: Make the Script Executable

1. Use the chmod command to grant execute permissions:

bash

chmod +x my_script.sh

2. Run the script:

bash

./my_script.sh

Output Example:

yaml

Hello, World!

Today is Mon Nov 23 12:00:00 UTC 2024

System uptime: up 2 hours, 15 minutes

12.3 Real-World Example: Automating Backups with a Shell Script

Scenario:

You need to automate the backup of a directory (/home/user/documents) to another location (/backup/documents).

Steps:

Step 1: Create the Script

1. Open a text editor to create the script:

   bash

   nano backup.sh

2. Add the following content:

   bash

   ```
   #!/bin/bash
   # Backup Script
   echo "Starting backup..."

   # Define source and destination directories
   SOURCE="/home/user/documents"
   DESTINATION="/backup/documents"

   # Create a timestamp
   TIMESTAMP=$(date +"%Y-%m-%d_%H-%M-%S")
   ```

```
# Backup command
tar -czvf $DESTINATION/backup_$TIMESTAMP.tar.gz
$SOURCE

echo "Backup completed successfully!"
```

Step 2: Make the Script Executable

bash

```
chmod +x backup.sh
```

Step 3: Run the Script

Execute the script:

bash

```
./backup.sh
```

Output Example:

```
Starting backup...
backup_2024-11-23_12-15-00.tar.gz
Backup completed successfully!
```

Step 4: Schedule the Script with Cron

139

1. Open the crontab editor:

bash

crontab -e

2. Add a cron job to run the script daily at midnight:

bash

0 0 * * * /path/to/backup.sh

12.4 Exercise: Create a Script to Display System Uptime and Disk Usage

Objective:

Write a shell script to display the system's uptime and disk usage.

Instructions:

1. **Create the Script File**:
    o Open a text editor:

    bash

    nano system_info.sh

2. **Add the Script Content**:

   bash

   ```
   #!/bin/bash
   # System Info Script
   echo "System Information"
   echo "-------------------"
   echo "System Uptime:"
   uptime -p
   echo
   echo "Disk Usage:"
   df -h
   ```

3. **Make the Script Executable**:

   bash

   ```
   chmod +x system_info.sh
   ```

4. **Run the Script**:

   bash

   ```
   ./system_info.sh
   ```

Output Example:

markdown

System Information

System Uptime:

up 3 hours, 22 minutes

Disk Usage:

Filesystem   Size Used Avail Use% Mounted on

/dev/sda1   100G 30G 70G 30% /

tmpfs   2.0G 1.5M 2.0G 1% /tmp

Tips for Shell Scripting

1. **Comment Your Code**:

   o   Add comments for clarity:

   bash

   # This script displays system information

2. **Test Incrementally**:

   o   Run the script frequently while developing to identify errors early.

3. **Use Variables**:

o Define reusable values:

bash

DIRECTORY="/home/user"

4. **Check for Errors**:
   o Use set -e to exit the script if any command fails.

5. **Debug Scripts**:
   o Run scripts in debug mode to trace execution:

bash

bash -x script.sh

This chapter introduced shell scripting, explained the basics of writing scripts, and demonstrated a real-world example of automating backups. Through hands-on exercises, you practiced creating and executing a simple script to display system information. Shell scripting is a powerful tool for automating repetitive tasks, improving efficiency, and enabling consistent workflows.

In the next chapter, you'll explore **Disk and Filesystem Management**, learning to monitor disk usage, mount and unmount drives, and manage file systems effectively.

CHAPTER 13: DISK AND FILESYSTEM MANAGEMENT

13.1 Introduction to Disk and Filesystem Management

Disk and filesystem management involves monitoring storage space, mounting and unmounting devices, and understanding the structure of storage in Linux. Effective disk management ensures that systems operate efficiently without running out of space or encountering performance issues.

13.2 Viewing Disk Usage

13.2.1 The df Command

The df command displays information about the disk space usage of mounted filesystems.

Syntax:

bash

df [options]

Common Options:

- -h: Display sizes in human-readable format (e.g., MB, GB).
- -T: Show filesystem type.

Examples:

- View overall disk usage:

  bash

  df -h

- Display filesystem types:

bash

df -T

Sample Output:

bash

Filesystem	Type	Size	Used	Avail	Use%	Mounted on
/dev/sda1	ext4	50G	20G	30G	40%	/
tmpfs	tmpfs	2.0G	1.5M	2.0G	1%	/dev/shm
/dev/sdb1	ext4	100G	60G	40G	60%	/data

13.2.2 The du Command

The du command estimates the disk space usage of files and directories.

Syntax:

bash

du [options] [path]

Common Options:

- -h: Human-readable sizes.
- -s: Summarize the total size of a directory.
- -a: Display sizes for all files.

Examples:

- Display the size of a directory:

  bash

  du -h /home/user

- Summarize the total size:

  bash

  du -sh /home/user

- List all files and directories with sizes:

  bash

  du -ah /home/user

Sample Output:

arduino

1.5M /home/user/documents/report.pdf

3.0G /home/user/videos

4.5G /home/user

13.3 Mounting and Unmounting Drives

13.3.1 The mount Command

The mount command attaches a storage device or partition to the filesystem.

Syntax:

bash

sudo mount [device] [mount_point]

Examples:

- Mount a partition:

  bash

  sudo mount /dev/sdb1 /mnt

- Mount with a specific filesystem type:

  bash

  sudo mount -t ext4 /dev/sdb1 /mnt

Viewing Mounted Filesystems:

- Use mount without arguments to list all mounted filesystems:

bash

mount

13.3.2 The umount Command

The umount command detaches a mounted device or partition.

Syntax:

bash

sudo umount [device | mount_point]

Examples:

- Unmount a device:

    bash

    sudo umount /dev/sdb1

- Unmount by mount point:

    bash

    sudo umount /mnt

Note: Ensure no files are being used from the device before unmounting. If a device is busy, use the lsof command to find open files:

bash

sudo lsof /mnt

13.4 Real-World Example: Checking Free Space Before Installing Software

Scenario:

You are preparing to install a software package that requires 10 GB of free space. Before proceeding, check the available disk space on your system.

Steps:

1. **Check Overall Disk Usage**:

   bash

   df -h

2. **Identify the Target Partition**:
   - o Locate the partition where the software will be installed (e.g., / or /var).

3. **Ensure Sufficient Free Space**:

   o Verify that at least 10 GB is available in the partition.

4. **Analyze Directory Sizes** (if space is insufficient):

   o Identify large directories using du:

   bash

   du -sh /var/*

5. **Clean Up Unnecessary Files**:

   o Use rm to delete unneeded files or directories:

   bash

   sudo rm -rf /var/tmp/old_logs

6. **Recheck Free Space**:

   bash

   df -h

13.5 Exercise: Mount an External Drive and List Its Contents

Objective:

Mount an external USB drive and view its contents.

Instructions:

1. **Connect the External Drive**:

    o Plug in a USB drive and identify it using the lsblk command:

    bash

    lsblk

2. **Sample Output**:

3. graphql

4.

5. NAME   MAJ:MIN RM   SIZE RO TYPE MOUNTPOINT

6. sda   8:0   0   500G 0 disk

7. └─sda1 8:1   0   500G 0 part /

8. sdb   8:16 1   16G 0 disk

9. └─sdb1 8:17 1   16G 0 part

    o Note the device name (e.g., /dev/sdb1).

10. **Create a Mount Point**:

    bash

    sudo mkdir /mnt/usb

11. **Mount the Drive**:

bash

sudo mount /dev/sdb1 /mnt/usb

12. **List the Drive's Contents**:

bash

ls -l /mnt/usb

13. **Unmount the Drive**:

bash

sudo umount /mnt/usb

13.6 Tips for Disk and Filesystem Management

1. **Monitor Disk Space Regularly**:
   o Use df to track overall usage and prevent running out of space.
2. **Find Large Files Quickly**:
   o Use find to locate files over a certain size:

   bash

find / -size +1G -exec ls -lh {} \;

3. **Optimize Disk Usage**:

   o   Clean up temporary files:

   bash

   sudo rm -rf /tmp/*

4. **Automate Backups Before Unmounting**:

   o   Create a backup script to copy important data before detaching drives.

5. **Mount Drives Permanently**:

   o   Edit the /etc/fstab file to automatically mount drives at boot.

This chapter covered essential disk management tools, including df and du for viewing disk usage and mount/umount for managing drives. You practiced mounting and unmounting an external drive and checking free space before software installation. Mastering these tools ensures effective storage management and system reliability.

In the next chapter, you'll explore **Cron Jobs and Automation**, learning how to schedule and automate tasks using the cron system.

CHAPTER 14: UNDERSTANDING CRON JOBS AND AUTOMATION

14.1 Basics of Cron and Crontab

What Is Cron?

Cron is a Linux utility used to schedule and automate repetitive tasks, such as backups, updates, and log maintenance. It runs in the background and executes predefined commands at specified intervals.

Key Components:

1. **Cron Daemon (crond)**:
   - The background service that handles task scheduling.
   - Automatically starts at boot on most systems.
2. **Crontab**:
   - A configuration file where scheduled tasks are defined.

Crontab Syntax:

Each line in a crontab file specifies:

bash

* * * * * command_to_execute

- - - - -

| | | | |

| | | | +---- Day of the week (0 - 7; Sunday = 0 or 7)

||| +------ Month (1 - 12)

|| +-------- Day of the month (1 - 31)

| +---------- Hour (0 - 23)

+------------ Minute (0 - 59)

14.2 Scheduling Tasks with Cron

Editing Crontab

To create or edit a user's crontab:

bash

crontab -e

- Each user has their own crontab file.
- Changes take effect immediately.

Listing Scheduled Cron Jobs

To view the current user's scheduled tasks:

bash

crontab -l

Examples of Cron Jobs:

1. **Run a Script Daily at Midnight**:

   bash

   ```
   0 0 * * * /path/to/script.sh
   ```

2. **Check Disk Usage Every Hour**:

   bash

   ```
   0 * * * * df -h > /path/to/disk_usage.log
   ```

3. **Clear Temporary Files Every Sunday at 2:00 AM**:

   bash

   ```
   0 2 * * 0 rm -rf /tmp/*
   ```

4. **Custom Intervals Using /**:
   - Every 5 minutes:

     bash

     ```
     */5 * * * * /path/to/script.sh
     ```

   - Every 2 hours:

     bash

0 */2 * * * /path/to/script.sh

14.3 Real-World Example: Scheduling a Daily Log Cleanup Script

Scenario:

You have a script (cleanup.sh) to delete logs older than 7 days, and you want it to run daily at midnight.

Steps:

1. **Create the Script**:

   bash

   nano /path/to/cleanup.sh
   Add the following:

   bash

   #!/bin/bash
   find /var/log -type f -mtime +7 -exec rm -f {} \;
   echo "Log cleanup completed on $(date)" >> /var/log/cleanup.log

o   This script deletes log files older than 7 days from /var/log.

2. **Make the Script Executable**:

bash

chmod +x /path/to/cleanup.sh

3. **Edit Crontab**:

bash

crontab -e
Add the following line:

bash

0 0 * * * /path/to/cleanup.sh

4. **Verify the Cron Job**:

o   List the user's scheduled tasks:

bash

crontab -l

5. **Monitor Execution**:

o   Check the /var/log/cleanup.log file for confirmation.

14.4 Exercise: Set Up a Cron Job to Back Up a Folder Every Sunday

Objective:

Create a cron job that backs up the /home/user/documents folder to /backup/documents every Sunday at 3:00 AM.

Instructions:

1. **Create the Backup Script**:

   bash

   nano /path/to/backup.sh
   Add the following:

   bash

   ```
   #!/bin/bash
   SOURCE="/home/user/documents"
   DESTINATION="/backup/documents"
   TIMESTAMP=$(date +"%Y-%m-%d_%H-%M-%S")
   tar -czvf $DESTINATION/backup_$TIMESTAMP.tar.gz $SOURCE
   echo "Backup completed on $(date)" >> /var/log/backup.log
   ```

2. **Make the Script Executable**:

bash

chmod +x /path/to/backup.sh

3. **Schedule the Cron Job**:
   - o Open crontab:

   bash

   crontab -e

   - o Add the following line:

   bash

   0 3 * * 0 /path/to/backup.sh

4. **Verify the Cron Job**:
   - o List scheduled tasks:

   bash

   crontab -l

5. **Test the Script**:
   - o Run the script manually to ensure it works:

bash

/path/to/backup.sh

6. **Monitor Execution**:
   - o Check the /var/log/backup.log file for backup completion messages.

14.5 Tips for Using Cron Effectively

1. **Redirect Output to Logs**:
   - o Capture standard output and errors:

   bash

   * * * * * /path/to/script.sh >> /path/to/logfile.log 2>&1

2. **Test Scripts Manually First**:
   - o Always test scripts by running them manually to ensure they work as expected.
3. **Use Absolute Paths**:
   - o Avoid relative paths in cron jobs to prevent errors.
4. **Monitor Cron Logs**:
   - o View cron logs for debugging:

bash

sudo grep CRON /var/log/syslog

5. **Schedule Resource-Intensive Jobs During Off-Peak Hours**:
   o Avoid scheduling CPU- or I/O-heavy tasks during peak usage times.

This chapter introduced cron jobs as a powerful way to automate recurring tasks in Linux. You learned how to create, edit, and monitor cron jobs, and applied this knowledge in real-world examples and exercises. Automating tasks with cron improves efficiency, reduces manual effort, and ensures consistency.

In the next chapter, you'll delve into **Managing Services and Daemons**, exploring how to start, stop, and configure system services using tools like systemctl.

CHAPTER 15: MANAGING SERVICES AND DAEMONS

15.1 Introduction to Services and Daemons

What Are Services and Daemons?

- **Services**:
    - Background processes that perform specific tasks or provide functionality, such as networking or web hosting.
    - Managed by a service manager like systemd.
- **Daemons**:
    - Long-running processes, often started at boot, that provide system-level or application-specific functions.
    - Common daemons include sshd (SSH), nginx (web server), and cron (scheduled tasks).

Managing services ensures system stability, performance, and functionality.

15.2 Managing Services with systemctl

The systemctl command is the primary tool for managing services on systemd-based systems.

15.2.1 Checking the Status of a Service

To view the status of a service:

bash

systemctl status service_name

Example:

bash

systemctl status nginx

Output:

css

• nginx.service - A high performance web server and a reverse proxy server

Loaded: loaded (/lib/systemd/system/nginx.service; enabled; vendor preset: enabled)

Active: active (running) since Mon 2024-11-23 10:00:00 UTC; 1h ago

15.2.2 Starting and Stopping Services

- Start a service:

bash

sudo systemctl start service_name

- Stop a service:

bash

sudo systemctl stop service_name

15.2.3 Restarting and Reloading Services

- Restart a service (stop and start):

bash

sudo systemctl restart service_name

- Reload a service configuration without stopping:

bash

sudo systemctl reload service_name

15.2.4 Enabling and Disabling Services

- Enable a service to start at boot:

bash

sudo systemctl enable service_name

- Disable a service from starting at boot:

bash

sudo systemctl disable service_name

15.3 Managing Services with service

The service command is an older tool for managing services but is still supported on many systems.

- Check the status of a service:

bash

sudo service service_name status

- Start a service:

bash

sudo service service_name start

- Stop a service:

bash

sudo service service_name stop

- Restart a service:

bash

sudo service service_name restart

15.4 Real-World Example: Restarting a Web Server After Updating Its Configuration

Scenario:

You've updated the configuration file for an nginx web server and need to restart it to apply the changes.

Steps:

1. **Edit the Configuration File**:
   - o   Open the nginx configuration file:

     bash

     sudo nano /etc/nginx/nginx.conf

   - o   Make the necessary changes, save, and exit.
2. **Check the Configuration Syntax**:

bash

sudo nginx -t

Output:

     o   If the configuration is valid:

vbnet

nginx: the configuration file /etc/nginx/nginx.conf syntax is ok

nginx: configuration file /etc/nginx/nginx.conf test is successful

3. **Reload the nginx Service**:

     o   Reload to apply the changes:

bash

sudo systemctl reload nginx

4. **Verify the Service Status**:

     o   Check that the service is running:

bash

systemctl status nginx

5. **Test the Web Server**:

   o Open a browser or use curl to confirm the changes:

   bash

   curl http://localhost

15.5 Exercise: Check the Status of a Specific Service and Restart It

Objective:

Check the status of the cron service and restart it if it is not active.

Instructions:

1. **Check the Status of cron**:

   bash

   systemctl status cron
   Expected Output:

   o If active:

   arduino

- cron.service - Regular background program processing daemon

  Active: active (running) since Mon 2024-11-23 09:00:00 UTC; 2h ago

o If inactive:

css

- cron.service - Regular background program processing daemon

  Active: inactive (dead) since Mon 2024-11-23 08:00:00 UTC; 3h ago

2. **Start or Restart the Service**:

   o If inactive, start the service:

   bash

   sudo systemctl start cron

   o If already running, restart the service:

   bash

   sudo systemctl restart cron

3. **Verify the Status**:

   o Check the status again to confirm:

   bash

   systemctl status cron

4. **Bonus Task**:

   o Enable the service to start at boot:

   bash

   sudo systemctl enable cron

15.6 Tips for Managing Services

1. **Use Logs for Debugging**:

   o View recent service logs:

   bash

   journalctl -u service_name

2. **Monitor Service Health**:

   o Automatically restart a failed service:

   bash

sudo systemctl enable --now service_name

3. **Disable Unused Services**:

o   Stop and disable unnecessary services to improve performance and security:

bash

sudo systemctl disable service_name

4. **Combine systemctl Commands**:

o   Use is-active or is-enabled to check service status:

bash

systemctl is-active service_name
systemctl is-enabled service_name

This chapter introduced you to managing Linux services and daemons using systemctl and service. You learned to start, stop, restart, and enable services, and applied this knowledge in a real-world example of managing an nginx web server. By mastering service management, you can maintain system stability and ensure critical applications are always running.

In the next chapter, you'll explore **Understanding and Managing Logs**, learning how to view and analyze system logs for troubleshooting and performance monitoring.

CHAPTER 16: UNDERSTANDING AND MANAGING LOGS

16.1 Introduction to System Logs

Logs are essential for monitoring system activity, diagnosing issues, and understanding system behavior. Linux provides several tools and directories for managing and analyzing logs.

16.2 Viewing and Monitoring System Logs

16.2.1 The dmesg Command

The dmesg command displays messages from the kernel ring buffer, which records hardware and system events.

Syntax:

bash

dmesg [options]
Common Options:

- -T: Show human-readable timestamps.
- --level=: Filter messages by priority (e.g., info, warn, err).

Examples:

- View the latest kernel messages:

    bash

dmesg

- Filter for errors:

bash

dmesg --level=err

- View timestamps:

bash

dmesg -T

16.2.2 The journalctl Command

The journalctl command is used to query and display logs maintained by systemd.

Syntax:

bash

journalctl [options]
Common Options:

- -e: Jump to the end of the log.
- -f: Follow new log entries in real-time.
- -u: Show logs for a specific service.
- --since and --until: Filter logs by time.

Examples:

- View all system logs:

bash

journalctl

- View logs for a specific service (e.g., nginx):

bash

journalctl -u nginx

- Follow logs in real-time:

bash

journalctl -f

- View logs from the past hour:

bash

journalctl --since "1 hour ago"

16.2.3 Logs in /var/log

The /var/log directory contains logs for the system and applications.

Common Log Files:

- /var/log/syslog or /var/log/messages: General system logs.
- /var/log/auth.log: Authentication and security-related logs.
- /var/log/dmesg: Kernel messages.
- /var/log/apache2/: Apache web server logs.

Examples:

- View the syslog:

bash

sudo less /var/log/syslog

- Search for specific entries:

bash

grep "error" /var/log/syslog

16.3 Real-World Example: Troubleshooting a Failed Application Startup

Scenario:

An application fails to start, and you need to identify the cause using system logs.

Steps:

1. **Check the Service Status**:

bash

sudo systemctl status myapp
Output:

yaml

- myapp.service - My Application
  Loaded: loaded (/etc/systemd/system/myapp.service; enabled; vendor preset: enabled)
  Active: failed (Result: exit-code) since Mon 2024-11-23 12:00:00 UTC; 2min ago

2. **View the Service Logs**:

bash

journalctl -u myapp
Output:

javascript

Nov 23 12:00:00 systemd[1]: Starting My Application...
Nov 23 12:00:01 myapp[1234]: Error: Missing
configuration file
Nov 23 12:00:01 systemd[1]: myapp.service: Failed with
result 'exit-code'.

3. **Check for Related Logs**:
   o   Search the syslog for related entries:

   bash

   grep "myapp" /var/log/syslog

4. **Fix the Issue**:
   o   Add the missing configuration file:

   bash

   sudo cp /backup/myapp.conf /etc/myapp/

5. **Restart the Application**:

bash

sudo systemctl restart myapp

6. **Verify the Application Status**:

bash

sudo systemctl status myapp

16.4 Exercise: Analyze Logs to Identify Common System Warnings

Objective:

Identify system warnings from logs and analyze them to determine their cause.

Instructions:

1. **View the Syslog**:

   bash

   sudo less /var/log/syslog

2. **Filter for Warnings**:
   o Use grep to search for warning messages:

      bash

      grep -i "warning" /var/log/syslog

3. **Analyze Kernel Messages**:
   o Check kernel logs for potential hardware issues:

      bash

      dmesg --level=warn

4. **Monitor Logs in Real-Time**:

   o   Use journalctl to follow new warnings as they occur:

bash

journalctl -f --priority=warning

5. **Take Action**:
   o   For each warning, research its meaning and apply corrective measures.
   o   Document the warnings and your actions for future reference.

16.5 Tips for Managing Logs

1. **Rotate Logs Regularly**:
   o   Use logrotate to prevent logs from consuming excessive disk space.
2. **Monitor Logs Automatically**:
   o   Use tools like logwatch or graylog for automated log analysis.
3. **Search Efficiently**:
   o   Combine grep with less for faster log analysis:

bash

grep "keyword" /var/log/syslog | less

4. **Use Filters in journalctl**:
   o   Filter logs by priority:

bash

journalctl --priority=err

5. **Archive Old Logs**:

    o   Compress and store old logs:

bash

tar -czvf logs_backup.tar.gz /var/log/*.log

This chapter introduced the tools and methods for managing Linux system logs using dmesg, journalctl, and the /var/log directory. You learned how to troubleshoot a failed application startup and practiced identifying system warnings through an exercise. Mastering log management is essential for maintaining system reliability and diagnosing issues effectively.

In the next chapter, you'll explore **Networking Tools and Troubleshooting**, learning to analyze and resolve network-related problems using tools like ping, traceroute, and netstat.

CHAPTER 17: NETWORKING TOOLS AND TROUBLESHOOTING

17.1 Introduction to Networking Tools

Networking tools are essential for diagnosing and troubleshooting connectivity issues, analyzing network traffic, and ensuring that systems are secure and accessible. This chapter introduces some of the most powerful tools available in Linux for network analysis and troubleshooting.

17.2 Networking Tools

17.2.1 netstat (Network Statistics)

The netstat command provides detailed information about network connections, routing tables, and interface statistics.

Syntax:

bash

netstat [options]

Common Options:

- -a: Show all connections (listening and non-listening).
- -t: Display TCP connections.

- -u: Display UDP connections.
- -n: Show numerical addresses instead of resolving hostnames.

Examples:

- View all active connections:

  bash

  netstat -an

- List listening TCP ports:

  bash

  netstat -tln

17.2.2 nmap (Network Mapper)

The nmap tool is a powerful network scanning and security auditing utility.

Syntax:

bash

nmap [options] [target]

Common Options:

- -sS: Perform a stealth (SYN) scan.
- -sU: Scan for UDP ports.
- -p: Specify ports to scan.
- -O: Detect the operating system.

Examples:

- Scan a single host for open ports:

  bash

  nmap 192.168.1.1

- Perform a detailed scan of a host:

  bash

  nmap -sS -O 192.168.1.1

- Scan a range of IPs:

  bash

  nmap 192.168.1.1-100

17.2.3 curl

The curl command is used to interact with web servers by sending HTTP requests and retrieving content.

Syntax:

bash

curl [options] [URL]

Common Options:

- -I: Fetch only HTTP headers.
- -O: Save the file to the current directory.
- -d: Send POST data.

Examples:

- Fetch a webpage:

    bash

    curl https://example.com

- Fetch only HTTP headers:

    bash

    curl -I https://example.com

- Download a file:

bash

curl -O https://example.com/file.txt

17.2.4 wget

The wget tool is a non-interactive utility for downloading files from the web.

Syntax:

bash

wget [options] [URL]

Common Options:

- -O: Specify an output file name.
- -r: Enable recursive downloading.
- -c: Continue a partially downloaded file.

Examples:

- Download a file:

bash

wget https://example.com/file.txt

- Download a file with a specific name:

bash

wget -O custom_name.txt https://example.com/file.txt

- Download a website recursively:

bash

wget -r https://example.com

17.3 Real-World Example: Testing the Availability of a Web Server

Scenario:

You need to verify whether a web server is online and serving content.

Steps:

1. **Ping the Server**:
   - o   Test basic connectivity:

   bash

ping -c 3 example.com

2. **Check TCP Connectivity with curl**:
   - o   Fetch HTTP headers:

   bash

   curl -I https://example.com

3. **Output**:
4. yaml
5.
6. HTTP/1.1 200 OK
7. Date: Mon, 23 Nov 2024 10:00:00 GMT
8. Server: nginx/1.18.0
9. **Use nmap to Scan Open Ports**:
   - o   Check if the HTTP port is open:

   bash

   nmap -p 80,443 example.com

10. **Use wget to Test File Download**:
   - o   Download the server's homepage:

   bash

wget https://example.com

11. **Verify the Download**:

    o   Check the contents of the downloaded file:

bash

cat index.html

17.4 Exercise: Use nmap to Scan for Open Ports on a System

Objective:

Perform a network scan using nmap to identify open ports on a specific system.

Instructions:

1. **Identify the Target System**:

    o   Use the ping command to ensure the target system is reachable:

bash

ping -c 3 192.168.1.100

2. **Perform a Basic Scan**:

    o   Run nmap to detect open ports:

bash

nmap 192.168.1.100

3. **Perform a Stealth Scan**:

    o   Use the SYN scan option:

bash

nmap -sS 192.168.1.100

4. **Scan a Range of Ports**:

    o   Specify a range of ports to scan:

bash

nmap -p 20-80 192.168.1.100

5. **Bonus Task**:

    o   Detect the operating system of the target:

bash

nmap -O 192.168.1.100

17.5 Tips for Networking Troubleshooting

1. **Start with Basic Connectivity**:
    o   Use ping or curl to confirm the target system is online.

2. **Monitor Network Traffic**:
    o   Use tools like iftop or tcpdump to capture and analyze network packets.

3. **Combine Tools**:
    o   Use nmap for port scanning and curl or wget to test specific services.

4. **Secure Open Ports**:
    o   Close unnecessary ports and services to reduce security risks:

    bash

    sudo ufw deny 22

5. **Automate Checks**:
    o   Schedule periodic scans with a cron job for proactive monitoring.

This chapter introduced powerful networking tools like netstat, nmap, curl, and wget, along with practical examples of their usage. You learned to test web server availability and performed a hands-on exercise scanning for open ports. Mastering these tools equips you to diagnose, troubleshoot, and secure Linux networks effectively.

In the next chapter, you'll explore **Introduction to Bash Scripting for Automation**, diving deeper into creating and running custom scripts to streamline administrative tasks.

CHAPTER 18: ADVANCED TEXT PROCESSING

18.1 Introduction to Text Processing

Text processing is an essential skill in Linux for extracting, transforming, and analyzing structured or unstructured data. Tools like awk, sed, cut, sort, and uniq allow users to manipulate text files efficiently.

18.2 Text Processing Commands

18.2.1 awk

awk is a powerful tool for pattern scanning and text processing.

Syntax:

bash

awk 'pattern {action}' file

Common Usage:

- {}: Define actions to perform on matching lines.
- $1, $2, ...: Refer to specific fields (columns).

Examples:

- Print the first column of a file:

bash

awk '{print $1}' file.txt

- Print lines where the second column matches "ERROR":

bash

awk '$2 == "ERROR" {print $0}' file.txt

18.2.2 sed

sed (stream editor) is used for searching, replacing, and transforming text.

Syntax:

bash

sed 's/pattern/replacement/' file

Examples:

- Replace "foo" with "bar" in a file:

bash

sed 's/foo/bar/' file.txt

- Remove all occurrences of "DEBUG" from a file:

  bash

  sed '/DEBUG/d' file.txt

18.2.3 cut

cut extracts specific fields or characters from text files.

Syntax:

bash

cut [options] file

Common Options:

- -d: Specify a delimiter.
- -f: Extract fields.
- -c: Extract specific characters.

Examples:

- Extract the second column of a comma-separated file:

  bash

cut -d, -f2 file.csv

- Extract the first five characters of each line:

bash

cut -c1-5 file.txt

18.2.4 sort

sort arranges lines in a text file in ascending or descending order.

Syntax:

bash

sort [options] file

Common Options:

- -r: Sort in reverse order.
- -n: Sort numerically.

Examples:

- Sort a file alphabetically:

bash

sort file.txt

- Sort a file numerically:

bash

sort -n file.txt

18.2.5 uniq

uniq filters out duplicate lines in a file. It is often used after sort.

Syntax:

bash

uniq [options] file

Common Options:

- -c: Count duplicate lines.

Examples:

- Remove duplicate lines:

bash

uniq file.txt

- Count duplicate lines:

bash

uniq -c file.txt

18.3 Real-World Example: Parsing and Reformatting Log Files

Scenario:

You need to extract error messages and their counts from a log file (/var/log/syslog) and reformat them for analysis.

Steps:

1. **Extract Lines Containing Errors**:

bash

grep "ERROR" /var/log/syslog > errors.log

2. **Extract the Timestamp and Message**:

bash

awk '{print $1, $2, $3, $5}' errors.log > formatted_errors.log

3. **Sort the Errors**:

bash

sort formatted_errors.log > sorted_errors.log

4. **Count Unique Errors**:

bash

uniq -c sorted_errors.log > error_summary.log

5. **View the Summary**:

bash

cat error_summary.log

Output Example:

less

3 Jan 01 12:00:00 CRON[1234]: ERROR: Job failed
5 Jan 01 13:00:00 nginx[5678]: ERROR: Connection timeout

18.4 Exercise: Extract Specific Fields from a CSV File and Sort Them

Objective:

Extract the second column (e.g., "Names") from a CSV file and sort it alphabetically.

Instructions:

1. **Create a Sample CSV File**:

   bash

   echo   -e
   "ID,Name,Score\n1,John,85\n2,Alice,90\n3,Bob,75"   >
   sample.csv

2. **Extract the Second Column**:

   bash

   cut -d, -f2 sample.csv > names.txt

3. **Sort the Names Alphabetically**:

   bash

   sort names.txt > sorted_names.txt

4. **View the Results**:

bash

cat sorted_names.txt

Output:

Alice

Bob

John

Name

5. **Bonus Task**:
   - ○ Remove the header line ("Name") from the sorted file:

   bash

   grep -v "Name" sorted_names.txt > final_names.txt

18.5 Tips for Advanced Text Processing

1. **Combine Tools**:
   - ○ Use pipelines to process text efficiently:

   bash

```
grep "ERROR" file.log | awk '{print $2, $3}' | sort |
uniq -c
```

2. **Use Regular Expressions**:
   o   With sed and awk, apply powerful pattern matching for complex text manipulations.

3. **Redirect Output**:
   o   Save the results of commands to files:

   bash

   ```
   awk '{print $1}' file.txt > output.txt
   ```

4. **Test with Sample Data**:
   o   Create small files for testing before applying commands to large datasets.

This chapter covered advanced text processing tools like awk, sed, cut, sort, and uniq. You learned how to manipulate, extract, and analyze text files, applied these skills to parse and reformat log files, and practiced with a CSV file exercise. These tools are invaluable for automating tasks, analyzing data, and managing logs in Linux environments.

In the next chapter, you'll explore **File Permissions and Access Control**, delving deeper into managing file security and access using advanced permission techniques.

CHAPTER 19: SECURITY BASICS AND HARDENING

19.1 Introduction to Security Basics

Security is a critical aspect of Linux system administration. Securing services, managing firewalls, and monitoring network traffic are essential for preventing unauthorized access and protecting sensitive data. This chapter introduces practical techniques to harden your Linux system.

19.2 Securing SSH

SSH (Secure Shell) is a widely used protocol for remote system access. By default, SSH configurations can expose vulnerabilities, so securing SSH is an essential first step in system hardening.

19.2.1 Changing the Default SSH Port

The default SSH port is 22, which is often targeted by automated attacks. Changing the port can reduce the likelihood of brute-force attacks.

Steps:

1. **Edit the SSH Configuration File**:

   bash

   sudo nano /etc/ssh/sshd_config

2. **Locate and Modify the Port Setting**:
   - o Find the line:

   bash

   #Port 22

   - o Uncomment it and change the port (e.g., 2222):

   yaml

   Port 2222

3. **Restart the SSH Service**:

   bash

sudo systemctl restart ssh

4. **Test the New Port**:

bash

ssh -p 2222 user@hostname

19.2.2 Disabling Root Login

Disabling root login via SSH enhances security by requiring users to authenticate with non-root accounts.

Steps:

1. **Edit the SSH Configuration File**:

bash

sudo nano /etc/ssh/sshd_config

2. **Disable Root Login**:
   o Find the line:

   bash

   PermitRootLogin yes

o Change it to:

perl

PermitRootLogin no

3. **Restart the SSH Service**:

bash

sudo systemctl restart ssh

4. **Verify Configuration**:

o Attempt to log in as root to confirm it's disabled:

bash

ssh root@hostname

o The connection should be denied.

19.3 Managing Firewalls

Firewalls control incoming and outgoing traffic, acting as a barrier between the system and potential threats.

19.3.1 Using ufw (Uncomplicated Firewall)

ufw is a simple tool for managing firewall rules.

Install UFW:

bash

sudo apt install ufw

Common Commands:

- Enable the firewall:

  bash

  sudo ufw enable

- Allow traffic on a specific port:

  bash

  sudo ufw allow 80

- Deny traffic on a port:

  bash

  sudo ufw deny 23

- View current rules:

bash

sudo ufw status

Example:

- Allow SSH on port 2222:

bash

sudo ufw allow 2222

19.3.2 Using iptables

iptables provides more advanced firewall configurations.

Common Commands:

- List rules:

bash

sudo iptables -L

- Allow traffic on port 80:

bash

sudo iptables -A INPUT -p tcp --dport 80 -j ACCEPT

- Block an IP address:

bash

sudo iptables -A INPUT -s 192.168.1.100 -j DROP

- Save and persist rules:

bash

sudo iptables-save > /etc/iptables/rules.v4

Example:

- Drop all traffic except SSH (port 2222):

bash

sudo iptables -P INPUT DROP
sudo iptables -A INPUT -p tcp --dport 2222 -j ACCEPT

19.4 Real-World Example: Blocking Unauthorized IP Addresses

Scenario:

You've detected unauthorized login attempts from the IP address 192.168.1.100. Block this IP address using ufw and iptables.

Blocking with UFW:

1. **Add a Rule to Deny Traffic**:

   bash

   sudo ufw deny from 192.168.1.100

2. **Reload UFW**:

   bash

   sudo ufw reload

3. **Verify the Rule**:

   bash

   sudo ufw status

Blocking with iptables:

1. **Drop Traffic from the IP Address**:

   bash

sudo iptables -A INPUT -s 192.168.1.100 -j DROP

2. **Verify the Rule**:

bash

sudo iptables -L

3. **Save the Rule**:

bash

sudo iptables-save > /etc/iptables/rules.v4

19.5 Exercise: Set Up Basic Firewall Rules Using UFW

Objective:

Create a basic firewall configuration that allows SSH on a custom port, HTTP traffic, and denies everything else.

Instructions:

1. **Enable UFW**:

bash

sudo ufw enable

2. **Allow SSH on Port 2222**:

bash

sudo ufw allow 2222

3. **Allow HTTP Traffic**:

bash

sudo ufw allow 80

4. **Deny All Other Incoming Traffic**:

bash

sudo ufw default deny incoming

5. **Allow All Outgoing Traffic**:

bash

sudo ufw default allow outgoing

6. **Verify the Rules**:

bash

sudo ufw status

7. **Bonus Task**:

   o Add a custom rule to allow traffic only from a specific IP (192.168.1.50):

   bash

   sudo ufw allow from 192.168.1.50

19.6 Tips for System Hardening

1. **Regularly Update Software**:

   o Apply updates to ensure vulnerabilities are patched:

   bash

   sudo apt update && sudo apt upgrade

2. **Monitor Logs for Unusual Activity**:

   o Use journalctl or /var/log/auth.log for SSH-related logs.

3. **Limit Access to Critical Ports**:

o   Only expose necessary ports to minimize the attack surface.

4. **Use Fail2Ban**:

o   Automatically block IPs with multiple failed login attempts:

bash

sudo apt install fail2ban

5. **Backup Configurations**:

o   Save firewall and SSH configurations before making changes.

This chapter introduced security fundamentals for hardening a Linux system, including securing SSH, managing firewalls with ufw and iptables, and blocking unauthorized IP addresses. You practiced configuring a basic firewall using ufw to allow essential traffic and deny all other connections. By applying these techniques, you can significantly enhance the security of your system.

In the next chapter, you'll explore **Linux Performance Monitoring**, learning to monitor and optimize system performance using tools like top, htop, and iotop.

CHAPTER 20: INTRODUCTION TO GIT AND VERSION CONTROL

20.1 What Is Git and Why Use Version Control?

What Is Git?

Git is a distributed version control system that tracks changes to files and enables collaboration among developers. It ensures every change is recorded, allowing users to roll back to previous versions, branch out to experiment, and merge code effectively.

Why Use Version Control?

- **Collaboration**: Multiple users can work on the same codebase without overwriting each other's work.

- **History**: Tracks the entire history of changes, providing accountability and transparency.
- **Backup**: Changes are stored locally and can be pushed to remote repositories for safekeeping.
- **Branching and Merging**: Experiment with new features without affecting the main project.

20.2 Installing and Configuring Git

20.2.1 Installing Git
On Debian/Ubuntu:

bash

sudo apt update
sudo apt install git
On CentOS/RHEL:

bash

sudo yum install git
Verify Installation:

bash

git --version

20.2.2 Configuring Git

Set up your name and email, which will be attached to your commits.

Commands:

bash

git config --global user.name "Your Name"
git config --global user.email "youremail@example.com"
Verify Configuration:

bash

git config --list

20.3 Basic Git Commands

20.3.1 Cloning a Repository

To create a local copy of a remote repository:

bash

git clone [repository_url]
Example:

bash

git clone https://github.com/user/project.git

20.3.2 Adding and Committing Changes

1. **Stage Changes**:
    - o   Add specific files:

        bash

        git add file.txt

    - o   Add all changes:

        bash

        git add .

2. **Commit Changes**:
    - o   Save a snapshot of the staged changes:

        bash

        git commit -m "Commit message"

20.3.3 Pushing Changes

To upload local commits to a remote repository:

bash

```
git push origin branch_name
```

Example:

bash

```
git push origin main
```

20.3.4 Pulling Changes

To download and integrate changes from a remote repository:

bash

```
git pull origin branch_name
```

Example:

bash

```
git pull origin main
```

20.4 Real-World Example: Version Controlling a Project Folder

Scenario:

You have a project folder on your local machine, and you want to track changes using Git.

Steps:

1. **Navigate to the Project Folder**:

   bash

   cd /path/to/project

2. **Initialize a Git Repository**:

   bash

   git init

3. **Add Files to the Repository**:

   bash

   git add .

4. **Commit the Changes**:

   bash

git commit -m "Initial commit"

5. **Connect to a Remote Repository**:

bash

git remote add origin https://github.com/user/project.git

6. **Push the Changes to the Remote Repository**:

bash

git push -u origin main

20.5 Exercise: Initialize a Git Repository and Make a Few Commits

Objective:

Create a Git repository, track changes to a sample project, and push it to a remote repository.

Instructions:

1. **Create a Sample Project Folder**:

bash

```
mkdir my_project
cd my_project
```

2. **Initialize a Git Repository**:

bash

```
git init
```

3. **Create a Sample File**:

bash

```
echo "Hello, World!" > hello.txt
```

4. **Add the File to Git**:

bash

```
git add hello.txt
```

5. **Commit the File**:

bash

```
git commit -m "Add hello.txt"
```

6. **Modify the File**:

bash

echo "This is a Git demo." >> hello.txt

7. **Stage and Commit the Changes**:

bash

git add hello.txt
git commit -m "Update hello.txt with a demo message"

8. **View Commit History**:

bash

git log

9. **Bonus Task**:
   - Create a GitHub repository and push the project to it:

   bash

   git   remote   add   origin
   https://github.com/yourusername/my_project.git
   git branch -M main
   git push -u origin main

20.6 Tips for Working with Git

1. **Check Status Frequently**:
   - View the status of your repository:

   bash

   git status

2. **Use .gitignore for Unwanted Files**:
   - Create a .gitignore file to exclude files or directories:

   bash

   *.log
   node_modules/
   .env

3. **Undo Mistakes**:
   - Unstage a file:

   bash

   git reset file.txt

   - Undo the last commit:

bash

git reset --soft HEAD~1

4. **Keep Commits Descriptive**:

   o Write clear and meaningful commit messages for better collaboration.

5. **Sync Regularly**:

   o Pull changes before pushing:

bash

git pull origin main

This chapter introduced Git, a fundamental tool for version control, and covered its installation, configuration, and basic commands. You applied this knowledge to version control a project folder and completed an exercise to practice initializing a Git repository and making commits. Git is a critical skill for collaboration, managing codebases, and maintaining a clear history of changes.

In the next chapter, you'll explore **Linux System Monitoring**, learning how to monitor processes, memory, and resource usage to maintain system performance and stability.

CHAPTER 21: TROUBLESHOOTING AND DEBUGGING

21.1 Introduction to Troubleshooting and Debugging

Linux troubleshooting and debugging involve systematically identifying, diagnosing, and resolving issues in the system. Common problems may arise from hardware failures, configuration errors, or faulty scripts. This chapter focuses on tools and strategies to address these challenges effectively.

21.2 Identifying and Solving Common Linux Issues

21.2.1 Common Linux Issues

1. **Permission Denied**:
   - o **Cause**: Insufficient permissions to execute a command or access a file.
   - o **Solution**:
     - ▪ Check file permissions:

       bash

       ls -l file

     - ▪ Modify permissions:

       bash

       chmod +x file

     - ▪ Use sudo for administrative commands.

2. **Command Not Found**:
   - o **Cause**: Command not installed or missing from the PATH.
   - o **Solution**:
     - ▪ Check the PATH environment variable:

       bash

       echo $PATH

- Install the command:

bash

sudo apt install package_name

3. **Disk Full**:
   o **Cause**: The disk is out of space.
   o **Solution**:
     - Check disk usage:

bash

df -h

     - Identify large files:

bash

du -sh /path/*

     - Remove unnecessary files.

4. **Network Unreachable**:
   o **Cause**: Network misconfiguration or downtime.
   o **Solution**:
     - Test connectivity:

bash

ping google.com

- Check network configuration:

bash

ip addr

21.2.2 Systematic Troubleshooting

1. **Identify the Problem**:
   - Use error messages and logs for clues:

   bash

   dmesg | tail
   journalctl -xe

2. **Isolate the Issue**:
   - Determine whether the problem is user-specific, system-wide, or network-related.
3. **Research the Error**:
   - Consult man pages or search online communities:

   bash

man command

4. **Test and Apply Fixes**:

   o Apply one fix at a time and verify the result.

21.3 Using strace and lsof for Debugging

21.3.1 strace

strace traces system calls made by a process and can reveal where an application is failing.

Syntax:

bash

strace [options] command

Common Options:

- -o: Write output to a file.
- -e: Filter specific system calls.

Examples:

- Trace a failing command:

bash

strace ls /nonexistent_directory

- Save output to a file:

bash

strace -o trace_output.txt ./script.sh

- Filter for file-related calls:

bash

strace -e open ./script.sh

21.3.2 lsof

lsof lists open files and can help identify which processes are using specific files or ports.

Syntax:

bash

lsof [options]

Common Options:

- -i: Show network connections.

- -p: List files opened by a specific process ID.

Examples:

- List all open files:

  bash

  lsof

- Identify processes using port 80:

  bash

  lsof -i :80

- Check files opened by a process:

  bash

  lsof -p 1234

21.4 Real-World Example: Debugging a Script That Fails to Execute

Scenario:

A script (backup.sh) fails to execute, displaying a generic "Command not found" error.

Steps:

1. **Check File Permissions**:

   bash

   ls -l backup.sh
   Output:

   csharp

   -rw-r--r-- 1 user group 1234 Nov 23 backup.sh

     o   File is not executable. Fix:

       bash

       chmod +x backup.sh

2. **Verify the Shebang Line**:
     o   Open the script:

       bash

nano backup.sh

- o Ensure the shebang line points to the correct interpreter (e.g., #!/bin/bash).

3. **Use strace to Debug**:

bash

strace ./backup.sh

- o Look for errors such as missing files or permission issues.

4. **Check for Missing Dependencies**:
   - o Use grep to find ENOENT (Error No Entry):

   bash

   strace ./backup.sh 2>&1 | grep ENOENT

   - o Install missing dependencies.

5. **Run the Script Again**:

bash

./backup.sh

21.5 Exercise: Use strace to Analyze a Failing Command

Objective:

Identify the cause of failure for a command using strace.

Instructions:

1. **Create a Failing Script**:

   bash

   echo -e "#!/bin/bash\ncat /nonexistent_file" > fail.sh
   chmod +x fail.sh

2. **Run the Script**:

   bash

   ./fail.sh

   o   Observe the error message: No such file or directory.

3. **Trace the Script Execution**:

   bash

   strace ./fail.sh

4. **Filter for Errors**:

bash

strace ./fail.sh 2>&1 | grep ENOENT

Output:

scss

open("/nonexistent_file", O_RDONLY) = -1 ENOENT (No such file or directory)

5. **Fix the Issue**:
   o   Create the missing file:

   bash

   touch /nonexistent_file

6. **Run the Script Again**:

bash

./fail.sh

21.6 Tips for Effective Debugging

1. **Use Logs**:
   - o System logs are invaluable for identifying issues:

   bash

   journalctl -xe

2. **Simplify the Problem**:
   - o Break down the failing command or script into smaller components.

3. **Monitor Resource Usage**:
   - o Use tools like top or iotop to detect resource-related bottlenecks.

4. **Document Solutions**:
   - o Record troubleshooting steps to save time in the future.

5. **Leverage Online Communities**:
   - o Sites like Stack Overflow and GitHub discussions often provide solutions.

This chapter covered practical tools and strategies for troubleshooting and debugging Linux systems. You explored common issues, used strace and lsof for debugging, and applied these techniques in real-world and hands-on exercises. Mastering these tools empowers you to diagnose and resolve problems effectively.

In the next chapter, you'll explore **Linux System Optimization**, focusing on techniques to improve performance and efficiency.

CHAPTER 22: TIPS, TRICKS, AND SHORTCUTS

22.1 Introduction

Linux is a highly customizable operating system, offering numerous tools to improve productivity. By leveraging aliases, keyboard shortcuts, and custom configurations, you can streamline workflows and save time on repetitive tasks.

22.2 Using Aliases to Speed Up Workflows

What Are Aliases?

Aliases are custom shortcuts for commands or sequences of commands. They allow you to define simpler or more intuitive names for frequently used commands.

22.2.1 Creating Aliases

Temporary Aliases:

- Create an alias that exists only for the current terminal session:

  bash

  alias ll='ls -la'

- Use the alias:

  bash

  ll

Permanent Aliases:

- Add aliases to your ~/.bashrc (or ~/.zshrc) file to make them persist across sessions:

bash

echo "alias ll='ls -la'" >> ~/.bashrc

- Reload the configuration:

bash

source ~/.bashrc

22.2.2 Examples of Useful Aliases

1. **System Monitoring**:

bash

alias meminfo='free -h'
alias cpuinfo='lscpu'

2. **Navigation**:

bash

alias ..='cd ..'

alias ...='cd ../..'

3. **Shortening Common Commands**:

bash

alias g='git'
alias gs='git status'

4. **Safety Enhancements**:

bash

alias rm='rm -i' # Prompt before removing files

5. **Custom Scripts**:
   o Create a script for frequently used tasks (e.g., backups) and alias it:

   bash

   alias backup='bash /path/to/backup.sh'

22.3 Navigating Efficiently with Keyboard Shortcuts

22.3.1 Command Line Navigation

- **Move the Cursor**:

  ○ Ctrl+A: Go to the beginning of the line.

  ○ Ctrl+E: Go to the end of the line.

  ○ Ctrl+U: Clear everything before the cursor.

  ○ Ctrl+K: Clear everything after the cursor.

- **Edit Commands**:

  ○ Ctrl+W: Delete the word before the cursor.

  ○ Ctrl+Y: Paste previously cut text.

- **Search Command History**:

  ○ Ctrl+R: Search backward in command history.

22.3.2 Terminal Management

- **Switch Between Tabs** (in terminal emulators like GNOME Terminal):

  ○ Ctrl+Shift+Tab or Ctrl+PageUp: Move to the previous tab.

  ○ Ctrl+Tab or Ctrl+PageDown: Move to the next tab.

- **Clear the Screen**:

  ○ Ctrl+L: Clear the terminal screen.

- **Suspend or Exit Processes**:

  ○ Ctrl+Z: Suspend a running process.

  ○ Ctrl+C: Interrupt (terminate) a running process.

22.3.3 File and Directory Navigation

- Use the Tab key for auto-completion of file or directory names:

bash

cd /usr/lo[TAB]
Expands to /usr/local.

- Quickly switch to the previous directory:

bash

cd -

22.4 Real-World Example: Customizing .bashrc for Productivity

Scenario:

You want to customize your terminal environment to streamline your daily tasks.

Steps:

1. **Open the .bashrc File**:

bash

nano ~/.bashrc

2. **Add Useful Aliases**:

bash

alias ll='ls -la'
alias gs='git status'
alias ..='cd ..'
alias serve='python3 -m http.server'

3. **Set a Custom Prompt**:
   o Add the following line to customize your terminal prompt:

   bash

   PS1='\[\e[32m\]\u@\h \[\e[33m\]\w\[\e[0m\] \$ '

   o This displays the username, hostname, and current working directory in colored text.

4. **Add Environment Variables**:
   o Set up paths for frequently used tools:

   bash

export PATH=$PATH:/path/to/custom/tools

5. **Reload the Configuration**:

bash

source ~/.bashrc

6. **Test Your Changes**:
   - o Use the new aliases and confirm the prompt change:

bash

ll
echo $PS1

22.5 Exercise: Create Aliases for Frequently Used Commands

Objective:

Set up custom aliases to simplify repetitive tasks.

Instructions:

1. **Choose Commands to Alias**:
   - o Identify commands you frequently use, such as:

```
bash
```

```
ls -la
git status
rm -i
```

2. **Create Temporary Aliases**:
   o   Run the following:

```
bash
```

```
alias ll='ls -la'
alias gs='git status'
alias rm='rm -i'
```

3. **Make the Aliases Permanent**:
   o   Add them to ~/.bashrc:

```
bash
```

```
echo "alias ll='ls -la'" >> ~/.bashrc
echo "alias gs='git status'" >> ~/.bashrc
echo "alias rm='rm -i'" >> ~/.bashrc
```

4. **Reload the Configuration**:

```
bash
```

source ~/.bashrc

5. **Test the Aliases**:

    o   Run:

    bash

    ll
    gs

6. **Bonus Task**:

    o   Create a custom alias to compress a directory:

    bash

    alias compress='tar -czvf'

    o   Use it to compress a folder:

    bash

    compress archive.tar.gz /path/to/folder

22.6 Tips for Productivity in Linux

1. **Use Command History**:

    o   Quickly repeat commands:

    bash

    !! # Repeats the last command

2. **Explore Keyboard Shortcuts**:
   - o Practice Ctrl combinations for faster command-line navigation.

3. **Organize .bashrc**:
   - o Group aliases, environment variables, and custom scripts for readability.

4. **Automate Routine Tasks**:
   - o Write scripts for complex workflows and alias them.

5. **Leverage Tools**:
   - o Install tools like fzf (fuzzy finder) for easier navigation.

This chapter introduced tips, tricks, and shortcuts to optimize workflows in Linux. You learned to use aliases, keyboard shortcuts, and customized .bashrc settings to boost productivity. By mastering these techniques, you can save time, reduce repetitive tasks, and create a more personalized terminal experience.

In the next chapter, you'll wrap up the book with a summary of key concepts and additional resources to continue your Linux learning journey.

www.ingramcontent.com/pod-product-compliance
Lightning Source LLC
LaVergne TN
LVHW052128070326
832902LV00039B/4132